YOUR PERSONAL

ASTROLOGY

GUIDE

ARIES
2013

YOUR PERSONAL

ASTROLOGY

GUIDE

ARIES
2013

RICK LEVINE **& JEFF** JAWER

STERLING ETHOS
New York

STERLING ETHOS
New York

An Imprint of Sterling Publishing
387 Park Avenue South
New York, NY 10016

ISBN 978-1-4027-7955-8

Distributed in Canada by Sterling Publishing
^c/o Canadian Manda Group, 165 Dufferin Street
Toronto, Ontario, Canada M6K 3H6
Distributed in the United Kingdom by GMC Distribution Services
Castle Place, 166 High Street, Lewes, East Sussex, England BN7 1XU
Distributed in Australia by Capricorn Link (Australia) Pty. Ltd.
P.O. Box 704, Windsor, NSW 2756, Australia

For information about custom editions, special sales, and premium and corporate purchases, please contact Sterling Special Sales at 800-805-5489 or specialsales@sterlingpublishing.com.

Manufactured in the United States of America

2 4 6 8 10 9 7 5 3 1

www.sterlingpublishing.com

TABLE OF CONTENTS

Author's Note:

Your Personal Astrology Guide uses the Tropical zodiac based on the seasons, not the constellations. This method of determining signs has been and continues to be the practice of Western astrologers for over 2,000 years. Aries, the beginning of the Tropical zodiac, starts on the first day of spring every year. Contrary to what you may have heard, no one's sign has changed, regardless of when you were born and the addition of a thirteenth sign is not relevant to Western astrology.

Measuring and recording the apparent movement of the Sun, the Moon, and the planets against the backdrop of the heavens is a complex task because nothing is stationary. Even the location of the constellations with respect to the seasons gradually changes from year to year. Since astrologers are concerned with human behavior here on Earth, they created a twelve-fold zodiac that is anchored to four seasons as their primary frame of reference. Obviously, astrologers fully understand that there are eighty-eight official constellations and that the moving planets travel through many of them (including Ophiuchus and Orion), but these are not—and never have been—part of the Tropical zodiac created by astrologers.

THE PURPOSE OF THIS BOOK

The more you learn about yourself, the better able you are to wisely use the energies in your life.
For more than 3,000 years, astrology has been the sharpest tool in the box for describing the human condition. Used by virtually every culture on the planet, astrology continues to serve as a link between individual lives and planetary cycles. We gain valuable insights into personal issues with a birth chart, and can plot the patterns of the year ahead in meaningful ways for individuals as well as groups. You share your sun sign with eight percent of humanity. Clearly, you're not all going to have the same day, even if the basic astrological cycles are the same. Your individual circumstances, the specific factors of your entire birth chart, and your own free will help you write your unique story.

The purpose of this book is to describe the energies of the Sun, Moon, and planets for the year ahead and help you create your future, rather than being a victim of it. We aim to facilitate your journey by showing you the turns ahead in the road of life and hopefully the best ways to navigate them.

YOU ARE THE STAR OF YOUR LIFE

It is not our goal to simply predict events. Rather, we are reporting the planetary energies—the cosmic weather in which you are living—so that you understand these conditions and know how to use them most effectively.

The power, though, isn't in the stars, but in your mind, your heart, and the choices that you make every day. Regardless of how strongly you are buffeted by the winds of change or bored by stagnation, you have many ways to view any situation. Learning about the energies of the Sun, Moon, and planets will both sharpen and widen your perspective, thereby giving you additional choices.

The language of astrology is a gift of awareness, not a rigid set of rules. It works best when blended with common sense, intuition, and self-trust. This is your life, and no one knows how to live it as well as you. Take what you need from this book and leave the rest. Although the planets set the stage for the year ahead, you're the writer, director, and star of your life and you can play the part in whatever way you choose. *Your Personal Astrology Guide* uses information about your sun sign to give you a better understanding of how the planetary waves will wash upon your shore. We each navigate our lives through time, and each moment has unique qualities. Astrology gives us the ability to describe the constantly changing timescape. For example, if you know the trajectory and the speed of an approaching storm, you can choose to delay a leisurely afternoon sail on the bay, thus avoiding an unpleasant situation.

By reading this book, you can improve your ability to align with the cosmic weather, the larger patterns that affect you day to day. You can become more effective by aligning with the cosmos and cocreating the year ahead with a better understanding of the energies around you.

Astrology doesn't provide quick fixes to life's complex issues. It doesn't offer neatly packed black-and-white answers in a world filled with an infinite variety of shapes and colors. It can, however, give you a much clearer picture of the invisible forces influencing your life.

ENERGY & EVENTS

Two sailboats can face the same gale yet travel in opposite directions as a result of how the sails are positioned. Similarly, how you respond to the energy of a particular set of circumstances may be more responsible for your fate than the given situation itself. We delineate the energetic winds for your year ahead, but your attitude shapes the unfolding events, and your responses alter your destiny.

This book emphasizes the positive, not because all is good, but because astrology shows us ways to transform even the power of a storm into beneficial results. Empowerment comes from learning to see the invisible energy patterns that impact the visible landscape as you fill in the details of your story every day on this spinning planet, orbited by the Moon, lit by the Sun, and colored by the nuances of the planets.

You are a unique point in an infinite galaxy of unlimited possibilities, and the choices that you make have consequences. So use this book in a most magical way to consciously improve your life.

MOON CHARTS

2013 NEW MOONS

Each New Moon marks the beginning of a cycle. In general, this is the best time to plant seeds for future growth. Use the days preceeding the New Moon to finish old business prior to starting what comes next. The focused mind can be quite sharp during this phase. Harness the potential of the New Moon by stating your intentions—out loud or in writing—for the weeks ahead. Hold these goals in your mind and help them grow to fruition through conscious actions as the Moon gains light during the following two weeks. In the chart below, the dates and times refer to when the Moon and Sun align in each zodiac sign (see p. 16), initiating a new lunar cycle.

DATE	TIME	SIGN
January 11	2:43 pm EST	Capricorn
February 10	2:20 am EST	Aquarius
March 11	3:51 pm EDT	Pisces
April 10	5:35 am EDT	Aries
May 9	8:28 pm EDT	Taurus (ECLIPSE)
June 8	11:56 am EDT	Gemini
July 8	3:14 am EDT	Cancer
August 6	5:50 pm EDT	Leo
September 5	7:36 am EDT	Virgo
October 4	8:34 pm EDT	Libra
November 3	7:49 am EST	Scorpio (ECLIPSE)
December 2	7:22 pm EST	Sagittarius

2013 FULL MOONS

The Full Moon reflects the light of the Sun as subjective feelings reflect the objective events of the day. Dreams seem bigger; moods feel stronger. Emotional waters run with deeper currents. This is the phase of culmination, a turning point in the energetic cycle. Now it's time to listen to the inner voices. Rather than starting new projects, the two weeks after the Full Moon are when we complete what we can and slow our outward expressions in anticipation of the next New Moon. In this chart, the dates and times refer to when the moon is opposite the sun in each zodiac sign, marking the emotional peak of each lunar cycle.

DATE	TIME	SIGN
January 26	11:38 pm EST	Leo
February 25	3:26 pm EST	Virgo
March 27	5:27 am EDT	Libra
April 25	3:57 pm EDT	Scorpio **(ECLIPSE)**
May 25	12:24 am EDT	Sagittarius
June 23	7:32 am EDT	Capricorn
July 22	2:15 pm EDT	Aquarius
August 20	9:44 pm EDT	Aquarius
September 19	7:12 am EDT	Pisces
October 18	7:37 pm EDT	Aries **(ECLIPSE)**
November 17	10:15 am EST	Taurus
December 17	4:28 am EST	Gemini

ASTROLOGY, YOU & THE WORLD

WELCOME TO YOUR SUN SIGN

The Sun, Moon, and Earth and all the planets lie within a plane called the **ecliptic** and move through a narrow band of stars made up by 12 constellations called the **zodiac**. The Earth revolves around the Sun once a year, but from our point of view, it appears that the Sun moves through each sign of the zodiac for one month. There are 12 months and astrologically there are 12 signs. The astrological months, however, do not match our calendar, and start between the 19th and 23rd of each month. Everyone is born to an astrological month, like being born in a room with a particular perspective of the world. Knowing your sun sign provides useful information about your personality and your future, but for a more detailed astrological analysis, a full birth chart calculation based on your precise date, time, and place of birth is necessary. Get your complete birth chart online at:

http://www.tarot.com/astrology/astroprofile

This book is about your zodiac sign. Your Sun in the fire sign of impulsive Aries lights up with zest when you feel free. Doing something new makes your adrenaline flow; you love that feeling of excitement and enthusiasm. You are in your element when the planets heat up the situations in your life. Although most other signs may feel quite comfortable when the cosmic weather cools off and produces comfort and stability, you tend to react with restlessness.

THE PLANETS

We refer to the Sun and Moon as planets. Don't worry; we do know about modern astronomy. Although the Sun is really a star and the Moon is a satellite, they are called planets for astrological purposes. The astrological planets are the Sun, the Moon, Mercury, Venus, Mars, Jupiter, Saturn, Chiron, Uranus, Neptune, and Pluto.

Your sun sign is the most obvious astrological placement, for the Sun returns to the same sign every year. But at the same time, the Moon is orbiting the Earth, changing signs every two and a third days. Mercury, Venus, and Mars each move through a sign in a few weeks to a few months.

Jupiter spends a whole year in a sign—and Pluto visits a sign for up to 30 years! The ever-changing positions of the planets alter the energetic terrain through which we travel. The planets are symbols; each has a particular range of meanings. For example, Venus is the goddess of love, but it really symbolizes beauty in a spectrum of experiences. Venus can represent romantic love, sensuality, the arts, or good food. It activates anything that we value, including personal possessions and even money. To our ancestors, the planets actually animated life on Earth. In this way of thinking, every beautiful flower contains the essence of Venus.

Each sign has a natural affinity to an individual planet, and as this planet moves through the sky, it sends messages of particular interest to people born under that sign. Your key or ruling planet is Mars, the Greek god of war. The angry red planet connects you with a primal energy that is not always combative. It's also very focused as it drives through life with an assertive competence that gets things started. Planets can be described by many different words, for the mythology of each is a rich tapestry. In this book we use a variety of words when talking about each planet in order to convey the most applicable meaning. The table below describes a few keywords for each planet, including the Sun and Moon.

PLANET	SYMBOL	KEYWORDS
Sun	☉	Consciousness, Will, Vitality
Moon	☽	Subconscious, Emotions, Habits
Mercury	☿	Communication, Thoughts, Transportation
Venus	♀	Desire, Love, Money, Values
Mars	♂	Action, Physical Energy, Drive
Jupiter	♃	Expansion, Growth, Optimism
Saturn	♄	Contraction, Maturity, Responsibility
Chiron	⚷	Healing, Pain, Subversion
Uranus	♅	Awakening, Unpredictable, Inventive
Neptune	♆	Imagination, Spirituality, Confusion
Pluto	♇	Passion, Intensity, Regeneration

HOUSES

Just as planets move through the signs of the zodiac, they also move through the houses in an individual chart. The 12 houses correspond to the 12 signs, but are individualized, based upon your sign. In this book we use Solar Houses, which place your sun sign in your 1st House. Therefore, when a planet enters a new sign it also enters a new house. If you know your exact time of birth, the rising sign determines the 1st House. You can learn your rising sign by entering your birth date at:

http://www.tarot.com/astrology/astroprofile

HOUSE	SIGN	KEYWORDS
1st House	Aries	Self, Appearance, Personality
2nd House	Taurus	Possessions, Values, Self-Worth
3rd House	Gemini	Communication, Siblings, Short Trips
4th House	Cancer	Home, Family, Roots
5th House	Leo	Love, Romance, Children, Play
6th House	Virgo	Work, Health, Daily Routines
7th House	Libra	Marriage, Relationships, Business Partners
8th House	Scorpio	Intimacy, Transformation, Shared Resources
9th House	Sagittarius	Travel, Higher Education, Philosophy
10th House	Capricorn	Career, Community, Ambition
11th House	Aquarius	Groups and Friends, Associations, Social Ideals
12th House	Pisces	Imagination, Spirituality, Secret Activities

ASPECTS

As the planets move through the sky in their various cycles, they form ever-changing angles with one another. Certain angles create significant geometric shapes. So, when two planets are 90 degrees apart, they conform to a square; 60 degrees of separation conforms to a sextile, or six-pointed star. Planets create **aspects** when they're at these special angles. Aspects explain how the individual symbolism of pairs of planets combine into an energetic pattern.

ASPECT	DEGREES	KEYWORD
Conjunction	0	Compression, Blending, Focus
Opposition	180	Tension, Awareness, Balance
Trine	120	Harmony, Free-Flowing, Ease
Square	90	Resistance, Stress, Dynamic Conflict
Quintile	72	Creativity, Metaphysical, Magic
Sextile	60	Support, Intelligent, Activating
Quincunx	150	Irritation, Annoyance, Adjustment

2013 GENERAL FORECAST

Astrology works for individuals, groups, and humanity as a whole. You will have your own story in 2013, but it will unfold along with seven billion other tales of human experience. We are each unique, yet our lives touch one another; our destinies are woven together by weather and war, by the economy, science, music, politics, religion, and all the other threads of life on planet Earth.

This astrological look at the major trends and planetary patterns for 2013 provides a framework for comprehending the potentials and challenges we face together, so that we can move forward with tolerance and respect as a community as we also fulfill our potential as individuals.

The astrological events used for this forecast are the transits of major planets Jupiter and Saturn, the retrograde cycles of Mercury, and the eclipses of the Sun and the Moon.

A NOTE ABOUT DATES IN THIS BOOK

All events are based upon the Eastern Time Zone of the United States. Because of local time differences, an event occurring just a few minutes after midnight in the East will actually happen the prior day in the rest of the country. Although the key dates are the exact dates of any particular alignment, some of you are so ready for certain things to happen that you can react to a transit a day or two before it is exact. And sometimes you can be so entrenched in habits or unwilling to change that you may not notice the effects right away. Allow extra time around each key date to feel the impact of any event.

JUPITER IN GEMINI:
LARGER THAN LIFE
June 11, 2012–June 25, 2013

Astrological tradition considers multifaceted Gemini an awkward place for truth-seeking Jupiter. We can be inundated with so much information that it's nearly impossible to see the forest for the trees. Jupiter's long-range vision may be obscured by a million and one ideas that scatter attention, diffusing the focus we need to achieve long-term goals. Yes, this mind-opening transit stirs curiosity about a wide variety of subjects—but it may be difficult to concentrate and gain in-depth knowledge in any one area if we're skimming the surface. Expansive Jupiter in communicative Gemini can also be quite verbose, valuing the volume of information more than its substance. Philosophical flexibility and mental versatility are gifts of this transit, while its less desirable qualities include inconsistency of beliefs and careless planning.

JUPITER IN CANCER:
FEELING IS BELIEVING
June 25, 2013–July 16, 2014

Philosophical Jupiter provides understanding through emotions during its stay in sensitive Cancer. We're likely to reject ideas that do not correspond to gut instincts, applying a subjective check against concepts that sound good but just don't feel right. Returning to traditional sources of wisdom and reconnecting with nature and family deepens our roots in the past to provide a needed sense of stability in these tumultuous times. Yet looking back for answers to today's questions has its limitations; conditions are changing so rapidly now that old rules no longer apply. We gain a sense of safety by relying on time-tested principles, but we may lose the potential for envisioning a creative new tomorrow by following these well-worn paths. The sentimental nature of Jupiter in Cancer favors familiar circles to unfamiliar. Given this transit's protective qualities, this makes it easier to justify closing the door to new people and experiences. Racism, nationalism, and religious and ethnic prejudices are more prevalent when mental gates close to outsiders. Yet Jupiter in nurturing Cancer, at its highest potential, helps us recognize the living nature of truth in an ever-growing spiral that draws upon the best of the old to nourish new goals and aspirations.

SATURN IN SCORPIO:
SHADOWBOXING
October 5, 2012–December 23, 2014
June 14, 2015–September 16, 2015

Responsible Saturn in formidable Scorpio tests our resolve. We are challenged to look into the dark corners of our psyches where fears about love, money, and mortality hide. It's tempting to turn away from these complicated subjects, yet the price of doing so is high because we are then controlled by unconscious impulses. Saturn in Scorpio reminds us that no one is entirely pure and simple. The complexities of giving and receiving affection, dealing with hidden desires, and working with manipulative people are numerous. But if we're willing to show up and do the work, Saturn also offers clarity and authority, enabling us to address these complicated matters. Taking responsibility for dark feelings doesn't mean that we must suppress them; it's a signal to engage them with patience rather than punishment. Personal and professional alliances work more effectively when we stop keeping secrets from ourselves. Finally, with Saturn in Scorpio we could see even more consolidation of financial institutions as a result of bad loans.

MERCURY RETROGRADES
February 23–March 17 in Pisces / June 26–July 20 in Cancer / October 21–November 10 in Scorpio

All true planets appear to move backward from time to time, because we view them from the moving platform of Earth. The most noticeable and regular retrograde periods are those of

Mercury, the communication planet. Occurring
three or four times a year for roughly three weeks
at a time, these are periods when difficulties with
details, travel, communication, and technical
matters are more common than usual.

Mercury's retrograde is often perceived as
negative, but you can make this cycle work
for you. Because personal and commercial
interactions are emphasized, you can actually
accomplish more than usual, especially if you
stay focused on what you need to complete
instead of initiating new projects. Still, you may
feel as if you're treading water—or worse, being
carried backward in an undertow of unfinished
business. Worry less about making progress
than about the quality of your work. Pay extra
attention to all your communication exchanges.
Avoiding misunderstandings and omissions is the
ideal way to minimize complications. Retrograde
Mercury is best used to tie up loose ends as you
review, redo, reconsider, and, in general, revisit
the past.

All three Mercury retrograde cycles occur in
emotional water signs this year. This can make
communication more difficult, because it's not

easy to translate feelings into words. Our potential loss of objectivity, as well, can lead to even more misunderstandings than usual. Thankfully, these three periods give us the chance to reconnect with our emotions, which can inspire new waves of creativity.

ECLIPSES
Solar: May 9 and November 3
Lunar: April 25, May 25, and October 18

Solar and Lunar Eclipses are special New and Full Moons that indicate significant changes for individuals and groups. They are powerful markers of events, with influences that can appear up to three months in advance and last up to six months afterward.

April 25, Lunar Eclipse in Scorpio: Sink or Swim
This Lunar Eclipse in passionate Scorpio tells us to let go of the past and start living in the present. Taskmaster Saturn's conjunction to the Moon, though, encourages a tenacious attitude that can keep us entangled in unrewarding relationships. Resentment, jealousy, and revenge aren't worth the effort they take to sustain. However, initiating

Mars is conjunct to the sensible Taurus Sun, which favors simplifying life and making a fresh start instead of trying to fix an unresolvable problem.

May 9, Solar Eclipse in Taurus: Trim the Fat
The cost of comfort may become so high that we have to let go of laziness or of some luxuries to make life more affordable. There's a self-indulgent side to Taurus, and with combative Mars and talkative Mercury joined with the Sun and Moon, we can find ourselves aggressively defending our behavior. Yet trying to justify standing still and holding on to what we have may only increase the steep price we pay later for resisting the purging we need now.

May 25, Lunar Eclipse in Sagittarius:
Life's an Adventure
An eclipse in farsighted Sagittarius reminds us to bring our attention back from some distant vision to focus on the here and now. We can discover alternative ways to make life work instead of acting as if there's only one road to fulfillment. Beliefs may not hold up in the face of changing

circumstances that require flexibility instead of certainty. Asking questions reveals options that multiply choices, creating confusion for some but freeing most of us from rigid thinking and excessive judgment.

October 18, Lunar Eclipse in Aries: No Man Is an Island

Life is not a solo voyage even when we're feeling all alone. This eclipse emphasizes the need to work with others and demands some degree of compromise and accommodation. It's better to sit on the fence, gather more information, and mull things over than to race ahead impulsively now. While it may seem that sharing feelings with others hinders progress, it garners us support that overcomes the isolation of not accepting advice and assistance.

November 3, Solar Eclipse in Scorpio: Baby Steps

Expect power struggles controlling Saturn's conjunction to this New Moon Eclipse. It's not easy to trust people—and sometimes it's just as difficult to trust ourselves. This eclipse, however, is about backing away from pressure, reducing intensity, and seeking peaceful moments in our lives. Recognizing the gifts that we're given every day can alleviate a profound feeling of hunger, perhaps even despair, through small moments of joy and pleasure.

THE BOTTOM LINE:
YELL FIRE!

The Mayan calendar may have turned over near the end of 2012, but the human story on this planet is far from complete. Nevertheless, we are still in the midst of a period of powerful change that began with the opposition of structural Saturn and explosive Uranus in late 2008, when we experienced the first wave of the worst financial crisis since the Great Depression, along with the subsequent election of Barack Obama. The year 2012 brought the first of seven tense squares between Uranus and transformational Pluto that will recur through 2015, shaking the very foundations of societies around the world. The volatile Uranus-Pluto square is exact on May 20 and November 1, April 21 and December 15, 2014, and March 16, 2015. The long-lasting connection between revolutionary Uranus and volcanic Pluto is already fomenting change on a grand scale, and this will continue for years to come.

It is tempting, though, to gaze back and seek to re-create the relative safety of the past. Joyful Jupiter's entry into cautious and conservative Cancer will bring waves of nostalgia for the "good old days," along with protectionist calls for stronger national borders. Yet the idea that we can return to the past is not a feasible one. The technological cats are out of the bag, and addressing environmental issues alone requires forward, not backward, thinking. Our challenge is to construct new realities based on bold visions and idealistic dreams of a world that does not yet exist. This takes courage in the face of confusion and confidence in the midst of chaos. It's tempting to call out to higher powers to rescue us from the consequences of our actions: suffering evokes cries for help. And yet we are capable of healing ourselves if we finally embrace the twenty-first century instead of retreating to mythical moments of an idealized past.

Inventive Uranus in pioneering Aries is opening new neural pathways that are reshaping our view of reality. Yes, we may encounter moments when thoughts are so strange that we may fear ourselves to be mad. But curious minds, flexible egos, and adaptable emotions allow us to glimpse a more enlightened, evolved, and competent humanity without breaking down. We are challenged to dance with the stranger who enters our heads with perceptions that don't readily fit into our existing intellectual framework. We must find new ways out of the dilemmas that we've created for ourselves. Embracing small discoveries and appreciating surprises are good training techniques: they prepare us to step up to the next level of human evolution and continue the remarkable journey of love and light on planet Earth.

Remember that all of these astrological events are part of the general cosmic weather of the year, but will affect us each differently based upon our individual astrological signs.

ARIES
AUGUST–DECEMBER
2012 OVERVIEW

A CHANGE WILL DO YOU GOOD

You may feel overwhelmed at times this month, but holding onto the status quo is not a viable option. You'll be better served if you actively work toward radical transformation rather than attempting to prevent it. On **August 1**, your optimism can lift your spirits when the futuristic Aquarius Full Moon harmonizes with jovial Jupiter. The Sun's cooperative sextile with Jupiter on **August 2** encourages your spontaneity, but you would be wise to fine-tune your plans prior to **August 8** while cerebral Mercury is still retrograde. Nevertheless, this is not a great time to make decisions about love, for Mercury in your 5th House of Romance forms an uncertain quincunx with deceptive Neptune on **August 4–11**.

Your frustration runs high in the middle of the month. Although the second occurrence of the intense Uranus-Pluto square isn't exact until **September 19**—the first was on **June 24**—the Sun's harsh rays stress this long-lasting configuration on **August 14–15**, illuminating troublesome issues. You might feel as if you're facing insurmountable resistance—and it's further agitated by contentious Mars conjuncting naysayer Saturn on the **15th**. The creative Leo New Moon on **August 17** cooperates with Saturn and Mars, however, enabling you to settle down, channel your energy, and regain control of your current situation. There is no easy escape from your responsibilities when the Sun enters hardworking Virgo and your 6th House of Employment on **August 22**, followed by Mars moving into intense Scorpio and your 8th House of Deep Sharing on **August 23**. Fortunately, you are able to draw energy from a deep reserve when powerful Pluto supports the Pisces Full Moon in your 12th House of Inner Peace on **August 31**.

WEDNESDAY 1 ★ ○ You won't know what's possible unless you try

---

THURSDAY 2 ★

FRIDAY 3 ★

SATURDAY 4

SUNDAY 5

MONDAY 6

TUESDAY 7

WEDNESDAY 8 ★ Let your feelings guide you now

THURSDAY 9 ★

FRIDAY 10 ★

SATURDAY 11 ★

SUNDAY 12

MONDAY 13

TUESDAY 14

WEDNESDAY 15 ★ SUPER NOVA DAYS Remain calm in the face of turmoil

---

THURSDAY 16 ★

FRIDAY 17 ★ ●

SATURDAY 18

SUNDAY 19 ★ Be on guard against your own arrogance

MONDAY 20 ★

TUESDAY 21

WEDNESDAY 22

THURSDAY 23

FRIDAY 24

SATURDAY 25

SUNDAY 26

MONDAY 27

TUESDAY 28

WEDNESDAY 29 ★ There may be unexpected consequences to your actions

---

THURSDAY 30 ★

FRIDAY 31 ★ ○

THE COST OF FREEDOM

You're tested this month when circumstances beyond your control thwart your pursuit of your heart's desire. With eclectic Uranus in your 1st House of Personality, you're in a long-term process of reclaiming your individuality. You could push so hard this month that you inadvertently become a threat to someone whom you really want as an ally. Your key planet, Mars the Warrior, is in passionate Scorpio and your 8th House of Transformation throughout the month, and he urges you to beat the drums of rebellion on **September 3–4** when he aspects Pluto and Uranus. The second of seven squares between Uranus and dark Pluto in your 10th House of Career is exact on **September 19**. The first one, on **June 24**, may have triggered your discontent, but the issues you face are complex and may not reach final resolution until the last Uranus-Pluto square on **March 16, 2015**.

The Virgo New Moon on **September 15** falls in your 6th House of Details, making this an ideal time to take small strategic steps on your great journey. Instead of making grandiose plans without substance, do something manageable that has lasting impact. But it becomes more challenging to maintain your composure on **September 20**, when communicator Mercury adds to the dynamic Uranus-Pluto tension. The Sun's entry into socially astute Libra on **September 22** is the Fall Equinox, and a time to balance your personal ambitions with those of a partner or workmate. The heat is on as intense aspects fuel the relationship pressure cooker right up through the fiery Aries Full Moon on the **29th**.

SATURDAY 1

SUNDAY 2

MONDAY 3 ★ Clear and direct communication is your best bet

TUESDAY 4 ★

WEDNESDAY 5 ★

THURSDAY 6

FRIDAY 7 ★ You will accomplish more if you can rein in your exuberance

SATURDAY 8 ★

SUNDAY 9 ★

MONDAY 10 ★

TUESDAY 11

WEDNESDAY 12 ★ You're ready to try something completely different

THURSDAY 13 ★

FRIDAY 14 ★

SATURDAY 15 ★ ●

SUNDAY 16 ★

MONDAY 17

TUESDAY 18 ★ Consider the impact of your words

WEDNESDAY 19 ★

THURSDAY 20 ★

FRIDAY 21

SATURDAY 22

SUNDAY 23

MONDAY 24

TUESDAY 25 ★ SUPER NOVA DAYS Your patience is tested

WEDNESDAY 26 ★

THURSDAY 27 ★

FRIDAY 28 ★

SATURDAY 29 ★ ○

SUNDAY 30

DREAM THE POSSIBLE DREAM

Recent relationship tensions and work pressures begin to ease as you distance yourself from last month's intensity and begin to let go of the past. Four planets change signs on **October 3–6**, focusing your intentions, intensifying your emotions, and encouraging you to look ahead rather than in the rearview mirror. Messenger Mercury delivers a much-needed reality check as it runs into authoritative Saturn on **October 5**, prior to both planets entering passionate Scorpio and your 8th House of Intimacy and Transformation. Your mind is churning with unfulfilled dreams when your ruling planet, Mars, enters inspirational Sagittarius and your 9th House of Faraway Places on **October 6**. Fortunately, several helpful aspects culminate with realistic Saturn smoothly trining wishful Neptune on **October 10**, allowing you to define the most significant themes of your fantasies and begin a manifestation cycle that continues as this aspect recurs through **July 19, 2013**.

By midmonth you're caught between two extremes and your frustration could tempt you to act without thinking. Don't be tricked into believing you can solve a complex problem with one quick move. Yes, the fair-minded Libra New Moon falls in your 7th House of Relationships on **October 15**, but you aren't feeling all that balanced because expansive Jupiter forms a stressful aspect with restrictive Saturn as well. Your enthusiasm for life grows when just-do-it Mars opposes farsighted Jupiter on **October 28** and intelligent Mercury enters your adventurous 9th House on **October 29**. This is a smart time to study a new subject or plan a trip, for the determined Taurus Full Moon, also on the **29th**, helps you bring your ideas to fruition.

MONDAY 1	
TUESDAY 2	
WEDNESDAY 3	
THURSDAY 4	
FRIDAY 5 ★	Serious relationship issues require your attention

SATURDAY 6 ★	
SUNDAY 7 ★	
MONDAY 8	
TUESDAY 9	
WEDNESDAY 10	
THURSDAY 11	
FRIDAY 12	
SATURDAY 13	
SUNDAY 14 ★	**SUPER NOVA DAYS** Observe sensible limits

MONDAY 15 ★ ●	
TUESDAY 16 ★	
WEDNESDAY 17	
THURSDAY 18	
FRIDAY 19	
SATURDAY 20	
SUNDAY 21	
MONDAY 22	
TUESDAY 23	
WEDNESDAY 24	
THURSDAY 25 ★	Stop, look, and listen before you proceed any farther

FRIDAY 26	
SATURDAY 27	
SUNDAY 28 ★	Act with common sense

MONDAY 29 ★ ○	
TUESDAY 30	
WEDNESDAY 31	

ANYTHING CAN HAPPEN

While the pressures of your business and personal relationships are unrelenting, intense cosmic forces this month have the power to turn coal into diamonds. The choice is yours. You can either sell yourself short and give up before you reach your goal, or dig deeply into the shadows of your soul and reaffirm your commitment to growth, excellence, and positive change. Until **November 16**, your key planet, Mars, is in hopeful Sagittarius and your 9th House of Big Ideas. Venus in your 7th House of Others attracts unstable relationships on **November 1–3** as she activates the epic Uranus-Pluto square that lingers into next year. Meanwhile bold Mars stirs up a bit of magic as he forms creative quintiles with ethereal Neptune and lovable Venus. It feels as if your fantasies can overtake reality, but your adventurous plans can unravel during trickster Mercury's retrograde phase **November 6–26**. Additionally, an intense Scorpio New Moon Eclipse in your 8th House of Transformation on **November 13** is a further indication that you must let go of self-limiting assumptions if you truly want to succeed.

It's even more difficult to manage the current tension between your need for security and your irrepressible restlessness after an awkward quincunx between conservative Saturn and uninhibited Uranus on **November 15**. You grow increasingly ambitious once Mars enters industrious Capricorn and your 10th House of Career on **November 16**, but might face unexpected reactions to your impetuous behavior on **November 23–27** when Mars aspects Uranus, Saturn, and Pluto. If you stand up for your beliefs, the transitional Gemini Full Moon Eclipse on **November 28** marks a culmination of your hard work and brings signs of welcome relief.

THURSDAY 1 ★ A sudden twist on the partnership path creates excitement

---

FRIDAY 2 ★

SATURDAY 3 ★

SUNDAY 4 ★

MONDAY 5

TUESDAY 6

WEDNESDAY 7

THURSDAY 8

FRIDAY 9 ★ Pleasure is within your reach

SATURDAY 10

SUNDAY 11

MONDAY 12

TUESDAY 13 ★ ● SUPER NOVA DAYS The stage is set for dramatic change

---

WEDNESDAY 14 ★

THURSDAY 15 ★

FRIDAY 16 ★

SATURDAY 17 ★

SUNDAY 18

MONDAY 19

TUESDAY 20

WEDNESDAY 21 ★ Taking decisive action can settle a matter

THURSDAY 22 ★

FRIDAY 23 ★

SATURDAY 24

SUNDAY 25

MONDAY 26 ★ Stand firm in your convictions

TUESDAY 27 ★

WEDNESDAY 28 ★ ○

THURSDAY 29 ★

FRIDAY 30

INTO THE WILD BLUE YONDER

Your challenge this month is to maintain a practical perspective on the opportunities that come your way. Propitious Jupiter continues its yearlong visit to your 3rd House of Information, presenting you with an endless stream of data—some vitally significant, some just noise. Jupiter becomes the focus of uncomfortable quincunxes from lover Venus and warrior Mars on the **December 1**, warping your perceptions and making it difficult to know how much confidence to place in your point of view. Everything seems bigger and better than it actually is when the Sun in extravagant Sagittarius opposes Jupiter from your 9th House of Big Ideas on **December 2**. Although the Sagittarius New Moon on **December 13** encourages you to take bold steps on your personal journey, its bothersome semisquare to doubting Saturn can put obstacles in your path.

It's tempting to tell a tall tale when messenger Mercury opposes Jupiter on **December 17**, followed by charming Venus on **December 22**. Jupiter forms additional quincunxes with Pluto and Saturn on **December 20–22**, this time revealing your tendency to be over-optimistic in your definition of success. Fortunately, responsible Saturn forms a cooperative sextile with manipulative Pluto on **December 26**, enabling you to manage your resources and effectively work toward completing your mission. The nurturing Cancer Full Moon on **December 28** brightens your 4th House of Home and Family, yet the magnetic Sun-Pluto conjunction on **December 30** indicates that your year won't end on a quiet note. But even when Venus and Mars, the cosmic lovers, quarrel on **December 31**, a brilliant Mars-Uranus sextile offers innovative solutions that accelerate the speed of change.

SATURDAY 1 ★ **SUPER NOVA DAYS** It's tough to establish limits

---

SUNDAY 2 ★

MONDAY 3

TUESDAY 4

WEDNESDAY 5

THURSDAY 6

FRIDAY 7

SATURDAY 8

SUNDAY 9

MONDAY 10 ★ Consider what makes the most sense before taking action

---

TUESDAY 11 ★

WEDNESDAY 12 ★

THURSDAY 13 ★ ●

FRIDAY 14

SATURDAY 15

SUNDAY 16 ★ Don't take on more than you should

MONDAY 17 ★

TUESDAY 18 ★

WEDNESDAY 19

THURSDAY 20

FRIDAY 21 ★ Incorporate the magic of your dreams into your plans

---

SATURDAY 22 ★

SUNDAY 23

MONDAY 24

TUESDAY 25

WEDNESDAY 26

THURSDAY 27

FRIDAY 28 ★ ○ Trust your instincts

SATURDAY 29 ★

SUNDAY 30 ★

MONDAY 31 ★

2013 HOROSCOPE

ARIES

MARCH 21–APRIL 19

OVERVIEW OF THE YEAR

Your sign is on the cutting edge of change due to a dramatic cycle that took hold when revolutionary Uranus settled into fiery Aries on March 11, 2011, staying until May 15, 2018. This electrifying planet will shake, rattle, and roll with surprises, breakthroughs, and discoveries that are bound to keep you on your toes. Fortunately, your pioneering sign is made for exploring new ideas and experiences that will lead everyone else into the future. You typically find change an exciting adventure, but sometimes it's uncomfortable for others to be prodded into letting go of stale habits and outdated concepts. **It's up to you to blaze trails into unfamiliar territory, and you will continue to do so this year.** There are, however, two key periods when you must exercise extreme caution: Rebellious Uranus slams into tense squares with punitive Pluto on May 20 and November 1. Your margin for error is reduced within a week of these dates, making radical moves dangerous. Carefully calculate potential consequences, because once you've taken action, there may be no going back. On the positive side, these powerful transits can intensify your efforts and provide the force you need to overcome stubborn obstacles.

You may not have to venture far to connect with new people and open your eyes to fresh ways of thinking. Expansive Jupiter is in clever Gemini and your 3rd House of Immediate Environment for the first half of the year, increasing curiosity, spurring spontaneous conversations, and brightening most days with little discoveries that put a knowing smile on your face. Philosophical Jupiter shifts into caring Cancer and your 4th House of Roots on June 25. A deeper understanding of the family patterns that have shaped your behavior helps you recognize unconscious beliefs that may be hindering your progress. Diving into the emotions in which these memories are buried can leave you feeling vulnerable, but the process can also reward you with newfound clarity about your aspirations and how to fulfill them.

It's especially important to uncover the motives and desires hidden deep in your psyche with scrupulous Saturn's presence in penetrating Scorpio and your 8th House of Intimacy. This relationship-transforming transit began in

October 2012 and will continue through 2014, testing your resolve when dealing with personal and professional partners. **The greatest challenge is to be honest with yourself about what you want and what you're willing to give to get it.** You probably prefer being relatively independent— not relying on others for much of anything. However, you can't discover the full potential of your relationships until after you realize that you can gain more love, money, and satisfaction by combining forces with passionate and powerful allies.

DOUBLE OR NOTHING

The transit of Saturn in your 8th House of Deep Sharing raises the stakes in your love life this year. If you're not totally committed to the relationship you're in, expect discontent to linger until you make some major changes. If you're single, be discriminating in your choice of companions, ruling out those individuals who can't take you as far as you want to go. Pleasure-seeking is pretty much out of the question when your ardent ruling planet, Mars, squares somber Saturn on January 7, but a fresh wave of excitement is coming with the warmth of spring. The Sun fires into irrepressible Aries on March 20 with flirty Venus following on the 21st, boosting your confidence and amplifying your sex appeal. Sassy Venus's conjunction with sexy Mars on April 7 is hot, hot, hot. Here's your chance to rekindle the spark with your current partner or jump into a new romance.

POTENT PARTNERSHIPS

Align yourself with powerful people this year; it could be the key to your success. It's better to work with a demanding individual who challenges you than with an easygoing person who lacks high standards. Saturn, the ruling planet of your 10th House of Career, forms favorable trines to visionary Jupiter on July 17 and December 12 that provide an ambitious, long-term picture of where you're going. These strategic aspects reward you for stepping back and planning your next move with patience and discipline, instead of rushing ahead with a poorly thought-out idea. Launching or expanding your own business is favored when lucky Jupiter crosses the bottom of your chart on June 25 and begins a six-year ascent toward a professional peak.

SAVE FOR A RAINY DAY

Manage your money carefully this year, because unexpected expenses or interruptions in your cash flow can put you in a tight spot. Your financial picture could suddenly change on March 28 when magnetic Venus and erratic Uranus join the Sun in impulsive Aries. Your hardworking planet, Mars, enters tight-fisted Taurus and your 2nd House of Income on April 20, making this a better time for saving money slowly than trying to make a fast buck. The intense Lunar Eclipse in your 8th House of Shared Resources on April 25 and a Solar Eclipse in your 2nd House on May 9 warn against reckless spending and unnecessary borrowing. If you need a loan for an emergency or you require an investment for your business, fight hard for the best terms you can get. It's better to scrape by with less and pay it off sooner than to get trapped in a long cycle of debt.

CLAIM YOUR POWER

A new diet or exercise routine can work wonders for you when muscular Mars travels through your 1st House of Physicality on March 12–April 20. If you're already in good shape, exploring alternative forms of movement and experimenting with foods you've never tried are clever ways to avoid boredom so you can maintain a healthy edge. October is a key month for attending to your well-being, because the Aries Lunar Eclipse on the 18th highlights the physical aspects of your sign. Burning the candle at both ends could wear you out quickly, so protect yourself by making sure to get enough rest. If you're dealing with nervous tension, simplify what you eat to regain stability and make your life seem less hectic. Avoid risky sports and pushing your body to extremes to keep yourself safe throughout this time.

BUILDING FROM THE GROUND UP

A new chapter opens in your domestic life on June 25, when generous Jupiter enters your 4th House of Security for a yearlong visit. If your home already feels confining, you may now be convinced the walls are closing in. To gain some space, you can start by eliminating clutter; physical renovations or a move to a new location could also solve this problem. The deeper issues, though, are psychological; you may need to confront feelings about your childhood that you thought were already put to rest. Reopening an old wound is not masochistic if it allows you to see the past with fresh eyes. As novelist Tom Robbins states, "It's never too late to have a happy childhood." Being kinder to yourself and accepting tenderness from those closest to you will establish a stronger and wider foundation upon which to build a more promising future.

HOME SWEET HOME

You don't have to travel far from home to feel like you're on an adventure this year. Jupiter, the ruler of your 9th House of Faraway Places, begins 2013 in your neighborly 3rd House, so you can find plenty of interesting ideas and exciting experiences right in your own backyard. The Sagittarius Lunar Eclipse rattles your 9th House on May 25, altering travel plans or interrupting your education. Yet the eclipsed Full Moon's trine to ingenious Uranus might redirect you in a more stimulating direction. Jupiter shifts into your familial 4th House on June 25, spurring interest in your origins. Consider scheduling a visit to your hometown or a trip to the country of your ancestors sometime over the next year.

HEAVEN ON EARTH

This could be a very important year in your spiritual life. The urge to pursue higher truth is nearly impossible to ignore when Mars travels through otherworldly Pisces and your 12th House of Divinity on February 1–March 12. In July, cosmic forces gather, giving you the discipline and inspiration to make your newfound faith last. On July 17, metaphysical Neptune aligns harmoniously with wise Jupiter and then forms the same favorable aspect with orderly Saturn on July 19. This rare Grand Water Trine unveils meaning and purpose that you can apply in concrete terms the rest of the year.

RICK & JEFF'S TIP FOR THE YEAR
Pace Yourself

You tend to rush things, Aries, perhaps because you lack self-confidence, or you're unconsciously convinced you'll never reach your goals. Yes, acting impulsively gives you an adrenaline rush that makes life feel more exciting. Just remember that operating at high speed and leaping without looking are unlikely to produce the lasting results you want now. Instead, work this year on cultivating patience and planning strategically for your future. Slowing down to enjoy life's sweet moments is good practice for learning to take your time as you attack life's bigger challenges.

JANUARY

SHARE AND SHARE ALIKE

You can get 2013 off to a good start if you focus on being a cooperative member of the community. Mars, your energetic ruling planet, spends all of January in freedom-loving Aquarius and your 11th House of Groups, challenging you to integrate your independent spirit with collective goals. It's no easy task to express your individuality while remaining a supportive team player; you must find a healthy balance between self-determination and accommodation. This dilemma may grow even more difficult when you see the most competitive people rewarded as sociable Venus enters ambitious Capricorn and your 10th House of Public Responsibility on **January 8**. The Capricorn New Moon on **January 11** puts issues of authority and power in the foreground, intensifying your desire to reach the top of the mountain. However, an inelegant aspect from expansive Jupiter to this Sun-Moon conjunction can tempt you to push others out of the way in your desire to get ahead.

The pendulum swings in a friendlier direction when brainy Mercury and the heart-centered Sun enter your 11th House of Community on

January 19. This extroverted trend receives a boost from the expressive Leo Full Moon in your 5th House of Fun and Games on **January 26**. You're ready to make a dramatic move in pursuit of love or to show off your creativity, but stern Saturn's square to the Moon reminds you to remain sensitive to others' limits. Still, your optimism grows thanks to joyous Jupiter's favorable aspects to this lunation. This giant planet of good fortune turns forward in your 3rd House of Communication on **January 30**, offering you ways to make new connections and promote your ideas.

KEEP IN MIND THIS MONTH

Sometimes your thinking is just too advanced for others to understand. Work to build a bridge from the old ways to your new vision so that your friends can get on board.

KEY DATES

★ **JANUARY 4**
supersize it

A friction-free trine between assertive Mars and adventurous Jupiter infuses you with enthusiasm and innovation. The mood-setting Moon enters the picture with trines to both planets, making this a perfect day for sharing your ideas with excitement while remaining sensitive to the needs of your audience.

SUPER NOVA DAY

★ **JANUARY 7**
shoulder to the wheel

You are being held to higher standards today with little margin for error as hard-driving Mars runs into a wall of resistance from a blocking square with obstinate Saturn. Purpose and discipline are essential. Deviating from the rules could produce immediate negative feedback. If you can patiently follow a well-defined plan, however, you can refine your skills and establish a strong foundation that provides enduring support for your long-term goals.

★ **JANUARY 14-16**

genius at work

You come up with unconventional solutions to problems at work on **January 14**, when clever Mercury in your 10th House of Career forms brilliant quintiles with conscientious Saturn and inventive Uranus. Yet your success can arouse jealousy or leave you feeling unfulfilled as appreciative Venus joins hungry Pluto in your 10th House on the **16th**. Take a deep look at your working relationships to find ways to repair them or discern which, if any, no longer meet your needs. This is also an opportune time to develop a neglected talent or an underutilized skill.

★ **JANUARY 20**

my way or the highway

Mars forms an edgy semisquare with unruly Uranus, increasing your originality while lessening your willingness to follow anyone else's lead. This transit may show you a shortcut or two, leaving you excited with the brilliance of your discoveries. Yet a distinct need to do things your own way can be disconcerting to those around you who have different agendas. Watch out for reckless behavior and sudden anger, which can undercut trust and dry up tender feelings. If you're unwilling to make compromises, you may be better off on your own.

★ JANUARY 26
proceed with purpose
Today you're tempted by indulgence—the dubious gift of a luxury-loving Venus-Jupiter sesquisquare. Yet the distractions of delight may be overpowered by a pressure-packed aspect between inexhaustible Mars and persistent Pluto that's useful for tackling daunting tasks. You have the strength and commitment to finally complete unfinished business. Cleaning up matters from the past is especially helpful because it supplies a constructive place to put your passion. Strong feelings of attraction or repulsion can rattle relationships, so it's wise to temper your reactions with a good dose of self-restraint.

FEBRUARY

FINDING FAITH

February is ideal for embarking on a spiritual quest—and you don't even have to leave home. The journey starts when Mars slips into magical Pisces and your 12th House of Soul Consciousness on **February 1**. Your potent ruling planet grows soft and tender in this dreamy part of your chart, which makes charging ahead with projects a bit more unappealing than usual. Investing time in metaphysical studies, prayer, and meditation allows you to take much-needed breaks from the demands of daily life and put your worldly ambitions in perspective. As cerebral Mercury shifts into your 12th House on **February 5**, you favor imagination over logic and intuition over reason. Mercury's conjunction with diaphanous Neptune on the **6th** diffuses your concentration and leads to confusing conversations, but it's bound to enhance your creativity.

Enjoy a fresh start with friends and colleagues on **February 10** with the Aquarius New Moon in your 11th House of Groups. If you've made commitments that no longer suit your needs, this lunation might motivate you to back out of them. The Sun's shift into gentle Pisces and your 12th House of Privacy on **February 18** takes you out of the spotlight or reduces your drive, yet it's a wonderful opportunity to recognize how much pleasure you receive from helping those less fortunate than you. A wave of compassion and forgiveness sweeps over you on the **21st** thanks to a solar conjunction with spiritual Neptune, dissolving any feelings of guilt and seeding future dreams. Mercury's retrograde turn on the **23rd** slows communication and muddles messages. But the industrious Virgo Full Moon in your 6th House of Work on the **25th** may reveal an unusual way to be more efficient on the job.

KEEP IN MIND THIS MONTH

The work that's most meaningful to you may be invisible to others, but it still can nourish your soul and restore your spirit in powerful ways.

KEY DATES

★ **FEBRUARY 4**
long and winding road
It's a mushy Monday with mobile Mars in a
wobbly conjunction with diffusive Neptune.
This is useful for acting with great tenderness,
following your feelings, or making a point in a
gentle manner. At the same time, it's easy to
wander off track, wasting time in pursuit of an
illusion or wearing yourself out by forcing an
issue that's not ripe for change. Avoid pushing
straight ahead when taking the scenic route
might save you time and energy in the
long run.

SUPER NOVA DAYS

★ **FEBRUARY 8–10**
watch your words
A hyperactive Mercury-Mars conjunction
on **February 8** energizes your thoughts and
conversations. Indeed, you may be reacting too
quickly to consider the impact of your words
and manner of expression. Some of what you
say can be brilliant and insightful while other

statements could provoke anger or lead to embarrassment. The day's edginess may leave you feeling off-balance and uncertain about when to push your message and when to keep your opinions to yourself. Taking a moment to organize your thoughts increases your chances of sharing something useful. You tend to shoot from the hip when Mercury and Mars square exaggerating Jupiter on **February 9–10**; watch out in case you misinterpret someone, overstate your case, or explode over petty issues. If you channel your passion into creative projects, though, you can tap into a virtually unlimited source of ideas.

★ **FEBRUARY 15–16**
cut to the chase
This is a very constructive period; you're working more efficiently than you were earlier in the month. Mars in poetic Pisces picks up some muscle with a beneficial sextile to potent Pluto on **February 15**. Instead of meandering around lost in uncertainty, this aspect helps you to gather force and direct it with power and purpose. Mars is strengthened by a trine from

responsible Saturn on the **16th**, adding a dose
of discipline that also favors productivity. Quiet
confidence gives you the clarity to simplify
problems and solve them with relative ease.

★ **FEBRUARY 25–26**
rapid recovery
Loving Venus moves into sentimental Pisces on
February 25, arousing romantic longing on the
same day that the analytical Virgo Full Moon
might also stir up insecurity in relationships.
Retrograde Mercury's second conjunction this
month with testy Mars on the **26th** could incite
you to fire off some harsh words or possibly
to feel like the target of someone else's
inappropriate aggression. Fortunately, Mars's
reasonable trine with the integrative North
Node of the Moon quickly shows you how to
repair damage and restore trust.

MARCH

THE RACE IS ON

You can feel the heat rising this month as three planets fire into spontaneous Aries, inspiring you to take bold action. Pioneering Mars leads the parade on **March 12**, followed by the illuminating Sun on the **20th** and alluring Venus on the **21st**. Your irrepressible urge for new experiences tempts you to take chances—and you're happiest living on the cutting edge anyway. Still, it's possible to try some risky things while maintaining a backup plan so that you have a safety net to catch you if you fall. Stabilizing Saturn's sextile with profound Pluto on **March 8**—the second in a series that began on **December 26, 2012**, and finishes on **September 21**—can connect you with powerful allies who help you set appropriate boundaries and maximize the return on your efforts. Overblown Jupiter's quincunx with Pluto on **March 29** signals the need to simplify your plans by eliminating extraneous activities.

On **March 11**, the imaginative Pisces New Moon in your metaphysical 12th House joins Venus, adding beauty to your inner life and inspiring artistic expression. Mental Mercury's direct turn on the **17th** begins to solidify ideas that have been floating around looking for a place to land. The Sun enters fearless Aries on **March 20**, the Vernal Equinox, marking the start of a new astrological year and amplifying your taste for adventure. It's time to face the music in relationships on **March 27** with purging Pluto squaring the peace-seeking Libra Full Moon in your 7th House of Partners. Your reward for emotional honesty is more clarity about what you need and what you're willing to pay for it.

KEEP IN MIND THIS MONTH

Give yourself permission to be a beginner when you try something new. Making mistakes is not a valid reason to give up if you're enjoying yourself and learning along the way.

KEY DATES

★ **MARCH 3**
quiet strength
Today you're able to cut through complexity
to get to the core of a stubborn problem,
with help from a subtle but powerful—and
creative—Mars-Pluto quintile. It's possible
now to take control of a situation without
exhausting yourself or coming across as overly
aggressive.

★ **MARCH 7**
against all odds
Resistance from others slows you down with
a stressful aspect between Mars and Saturn.
If you are precise about what you want and
modest in your goals, you can earn the support
of a cautious person. But even if someone fails
to cooperate with you, a brilliant Mars-Jupiter
quintile could show you how to leap over
an obstacle by approaching it from a totally
different angle.

★ **MARCH 11–12**
you're number one
The inspirational Pisces New Moon on
March 11 stirs dreams of love and creativity
that might feel beyond your reach. But warrior
Mars enters courageous Aries the next day,
awakening your passion that can drive you
to succeed. Use it to pursue your goals, both
personal and professional; you have more
to gain by applying this intensity to your own
interests than by following someone else's
lead. Playing second fiddle or simply trying to
hold your ground may feel so confining that
your frustration ignites a conflict.

SUPER NOVA DAYS

★ **MARCH 20–22**
lightning in a bottle
You're filled with power and grace when the
Sun's shift into confident Aries and your 1st
House of Personality on **March 20** is followed
by charming Venus on the **21st**. All eyes are
turned in your direction as you shine your light
with charisma and passion. But watch out,
because dynamic Mars hooks up with wired

Uranus on the **22nd**, shocking you with a jolt of electricity that turns a cool situation into an inferno of activity. Restlessness and rebellion could lead you to act impulsively, unsettling those around you. Still, this is also a highly inventive alignment that can be super-sexy when you experiment with new methods or unusual looks.

★ **MARCH 25–28**
   liberation days
   Practice patience on **March 25** to handle rowdy Mars's quincunx to restrictive Saturn. Even if your enthusiasm rises with a high-octane Mars-Jupiter sextile on the **26th**, a Mars-Pluto square on the same day means you're better off concentrating on one task than spreading yourself too thin. The Sun and Venus conjoin Uranus on **March 28**, kicking up an urgent desire for freedom, and change leaves you teetering on the edge between genius and chaos.

APRIL

HIT THE GROUND RUNNING

Get excited about the first half of April because its cosmic energy can lift you to a higher level of happiness. The uncontainable Aries New Moon on **April 10** is an annual conjunction of the Sun and Moon in your sign, which usually brings a boost of energy and enthusiasm—and this one offers even more. Vivacious Venus and macho Mars join this New Moon, emphasizing playfulness, sex appeal, and creativity. This quartet of planets combines sensitivity with an inner fire that could make you more enchanting to others. But check your impulses when serious Saturn forms a constraining quincunx with spontaneous Uranus on **April 12**, the second of three aspects that began on **November 15, 2012**, and finishes on **October 5**. You may be expecting unanimous support for your escapades, but are more likely to be held back by a close friend or partner whose common sense exceeds your own.

Stability arrives with Venus's move into earthy Taurus and your 2nd House of Self-Worth on **April 15**, followed by the Sun on the **19th** and Mars on the **20th**. Slowing down to calculate expenditures of money and energy not only enables you to conserve now, but can lead to greater returns later. You may be surprised how much pleasure it brings to leisurely savor what you already have instead of racing toward the next object of desire. Responsible Saturn's conjunction with the relentless Scorpio Full Moon in your 8th House of Deep Sharing on **April 25** is further reminder to proceed with caution and respect the limits of others.

KEEP IN MIND THIS MONTH

Putting your energy into cultivating the relationships and activities that have long-term value ensures that you will get to keep the best things that come your way.

KEY DATES

★ **APRIL 1**
the power of your convictions
You'll arouse enthusiasm in others today if
you believe in what you say. The energetic
Aries Sun's harmonious sextile with optimistic
Jupiter expands your visions and empowers
your words. If you speak from your heart, then
you should have little difficulty connecting with
positive people who encourage your growth.

★ **APRIL 6–7**
field of dreams
You're living in either a state of grace or a
world of illusion during these romantically
charged days. Astrology's cosmic lovers, Venus
and Mars, form sketchy semisquares with
dreamy Neptune on **April 6** that can inspire
desire and stimulate imagination. The upside
of these transits is the sensitivity they bring to
your relationships, giving you more compassion
toward others. But on the downside, you could
get lost in the fog of fantasy. Venus and Mars
hook up in your sign on the **7th**, blessing you

with the magic of attraction. Your confident charm enchants others to give you what you want, but you can also be content to enjoy the beauty of nature and art or be transported by the magic of music.

★ **APRIL 13**
mind on the run
Messenger Mercury races into impetuous Aries to speed up your thinking and sharpen your mind. This is excellent for seeing the world with fresh eyes, discovering ideas and perspectives you never noticed before. Original concepts pop up quickly—and could burn out just as fast. Improvising is good in a pinch, but might lead to saying things that you regret. If you're dealing with a serious issue, reflect and do some research before making important statements.

SUPER NOVA DAY

★ **APRIL 17**
in the zone
You are an unstoppable human laser beam today with the all-powerful Sun-Mars

conjunction in aggressive Aries. This is a
fireball of energy that triggers you to take
immediate action. It helps if you already have
a project you're trying to get off the ground or a
new experience in which to pour your heart
and soul. When you have a racetrack to run on,
you could be unbeatable, but if you're dealing
with a humdrum day, your temper could get
the best of you.

★ **APRIL 26**
gentle persuasion
Adopt a softer approach to taking care of
business today with instinctive Mars in a
sweet sextile to compassionate Neptune. You
instinctively know how to cajole people playfully
instead of pushing them too hard. It's also
beneficial to be less forceful with yourself,
since tuning into your environment and
catching the currents can take you where you
want to go with less effort.

MAY

ON SHAKY GROUND

A pair of powerful eclipses this month takes you right to the precipice of change. On **May 9**, a Solar Eclipse in stubborn Taurus falls in your 2nd House of Resources, raising questions about finances and self-worth. If you've been sticking to an unrewarding job or investing too much in materials or skills that aren't paying off, it may be time to reassess your economic decisions. A Lunar Eclipse in adventurous Sagittarius on **May 25** rattles your 9th House of Travel and Higher Education. A stressful square to the Moon from imaginative Neptune can arouse fantasies of escape. Idealizing a place from your past might provide some inspiration, but it's more likely to distract you from discovering new ways to explore the world and broaden your mind. Yet even if you have your head in the clouds, your feet should remain on the ground when brainy Mercury travels through easygoing Taurus and your 2nd House on **May 1–15**.

Curiosity and flirtatiousness are part of the package when friendly Venus dances into lighthearted Gemini and your chatty 3rd House on **May 9**. You're more likely to appreciate people and activities in small doses now; boredom can set in very quickly. Mercury enters your 3rd House of Information on the **15th**, as does the Sun on the **20th**, brightening your days with a variety of experiences and people. Your willingness to talk about anything with just about anyone is excellent for opening new channels of communication. Just make sure that you're dealing with people who really understand a subject before you put your faith in what they say. Mars bounces into airy Gemini and Mercury swims into watery Cancer on the **31st**, encouraging casual behavior and subjective thinking.

KEEP IN MIND THIS MONTH

*You might find unfamiliar people and experiences
so compelling that you (incorrectly) assume they
will always intrigue you. Enjoy the moment
without trying to make it last.*

KEY DATES

★ **MAY 1**
shoulder to the wheel

Maintain a steady pace and focus on one job at a time if you hope to turn this frustrating day into a productive one. Active Mars's opposition to strict Saturn demands that you stick to a plan and not wander off track with clever improvisations. You have almost no room for error—and you will be reminded of this fact very quickly if you deviate from what's expected of you. Yet patiently attending to the toughest task can earn you some well-deserved respect.

SUPER NOVA DAYS

★ **MAY 5–7**
don't back down

A Mercury-Saturn opposition on **May 5** could lead you into a confrontation with a negative person. Don't take no for an answer now since a potent Mars-Pluto trine gives you power and efficiency to overcome most obstacles. On **May 7**, you're filled with moneymaking ideas as a perceptive Mercury-Mars conjunction in your 2nd House of Resources urges you to fight for what you believe in with a combination of strength and persistence that's hard to resist. Your perspective is likely to prevail if your argument is based on reliable information.

★ **MAY 13**
dazed and confused
Your emotions overcome your reason today as evaluating Venus forms a challenging square with fuzzy Neptune. Mars's conjunction with the karmic South Node of the Moon in Taurus provokes obstinate behavior when more creative perspectives are possible. A clever quintile between Mars and Neptune suggests that you may have more options at your disposal than you realize.

★ **MAY 20**
work in progress
Two major outer planet aspects suggest that deeper changes are brewing. The last of three Jupiter-Saturn sesquisquares and the third of seven Uranus-Pluto squares lead you to adjust your long-range plans, especially those

related to your career. Avoid rash decisions; external conditions are still in flux. Fortunately, the Sun's shift into adaptable Gemini indicates that there is more information coming. Remain flexible now until things settle down rather than forcing a showdown.

★ **MAY 25–26**
quick-change artist
The fiery Sagittarius Lunar Eclipse on **May 25** supercharges the day while a stressful Mars-Pluto alignment intensifies the energy. The eclipse invites escapism, but Mars-Pluto plays for keeps. This is not the moment to fight; you may be standing on shifting ground. A squishy Sun-Neptune square on the **26th** is better suited for daydreaming than for arguing. Additionally, an excitable Mars-Uranus semisquare incites you to lash out against targets that aren't worthy of your attention. Adapting swiftly to suddenly changing circumstances works better than holding tightly to a rigid plan.

JUNE

BACK TO BASICS

The buzz you're feeling when June begins is likely to have you moving in many directions. Your ruling planet, Mars, along with the Sun in jumpy Gemini incite you to flit restlessly from one activity to another. There's a subtle shift toward a more contemplative mood when lovely Venus enters caring Cancer and your 4th House of Home and Family on **June 2**. Nostalgia and domestic concerns pull on your heartstrings, leaving you more vulnerable. The jittery Gemini New Moon on the **8th** falls in your 3rd House of Communication, opening your mind to diverse people and subjects while increasing your distractions. On **June 11**, a subtle stabilizing force is the second of three trines between conscientious Saturn and idealistic Neptune that occurred on **October 10, 2012**, and will reoccur on **July 19**. Listen to an experienced individual whose hard-nosed pragmatism might help you make a dream come true.

Security is a top priority when the Sun shifts into protective Cancer on **June 21**, marking the Summer Solstice in your 4th House of Roots. Advancing your interests cautiously feels painfully ineffective, but it's healthier than forcing issues right now in your personal or professional life. The aspiring Capricorn Full Moon in your 10th House of Career on **June 23** could trigger a work-related crisis, yet is meant to highlight your long-term goals and push you to recognize the need for self-discipline. Lucky Jupiter's move into nurturing Cancer on the **25th** enriches your family life and encourages psychological development in the year ahead. However, it may take time to reach a deeper understanding of your desires, especially with fact-based Mercury turning retrograde on the **26th**. You'll need to do some backtracking before you are free to forge ahead.

KEEP IN MIND THIS MONTH

You can't control what happens in the world, but you do have many options about how you manage your emotions. Attending to your inner needs makes everything else easier to handle.

KEY DATES

SUPER NOVA DAYS

★ **JUNE 7-8**
scenic detour
You might drift off course on **June 7** when a fuzzy Mars-Neptune square favors fantasy and sacrifice over reason and ambition. Acting with compassion and tapping into your imagination are desirable expressions of this tender transit. Although the antsy Gemini New Moon on the **8th** says *go*, a balky quincunx between forward-moving Mars and stand-still Saturn can block your progress. The point is not to stop completely, but to redirect your efforts. If you encounter resistance, don't continue to push ahead or get bogged down in a battle. Navigating around (or adjusting your methods and expectations) is actually the most efficient way to get where you want to go.

★ **JUNE 15-17**
light at the end of the tunnel
Mars in flighty Gemini likes to let you wander freely, but your ruling planet's clunky quincunx

with fierce Pluto may extract a heavy price on **June 15**. Anger simmering below your surface could undermine a relationship—or erupt. Direct your attention to a single issue or emotion so you can address it with as much clarity and self-control as possible. Cleaning up clutter and finishing off minor tasks are beneficial ways to use this nervous energy. Pressure drops on the **17th** when Mars slides into an easy sextile with unconventional Uranus. This dynamic duo offers a sense of freedom that lets your intuition flow and your creativity shine.

★ **JUNE 19–21**
home sweet home
Your brain is bursting with ideas and your inbox is overflowing with messages when the Sun joins boundless Jupiter on **June 19**. This expansive event in your 3rd House of Information adds enthusiasm to your words and enhances your capacity for learning. Verbal Mercury's conjunction with affectionate Venus on the **20th** is in your private 4th House, creating an excellent moment for discussing

personal matters with care and tenderness.
The Sun's sweep into this intimate part of your
chart on the **21st** lights the home fires and
instills a sense of belonging that makes you
feel more secure.

★ **JUNE 27-28**
all the world's your stage
Stylish Venus sashays into loud Leo and your
5th House of Romance on **June 27** to lift your
spirits and raise your personal profile. Your
playful spirit and warmhearted generosity
make you and whatever you propose more
appealing. Recognizing the limits of others,
though, is essential for avoiding stress when
Mars tangles with authoritative Saturn on
the **28th**.

JULY

STAIRWAY TO HEAVEN

You reach a more profound understanding of your life's purpose this month with a rare Grand Water Trine flooding your most sensitive houses. Philosophical Jupiter in your 4th House of Roots aligns harmoniously with pragmatic Saturn in your 8th House of Intimacy and metaphysical Neptune in your 12th House of Spirituality on **July 17–19**, giving you a broader vision of your past that helps you map out a clearer picture of the future. Your key planet, Mars, joins this planetary pattern on the **20th**, enabling you to turn these insights into constructive action. There are, though, some hurdles and some helpers along the way. The Sun's opposition to powerful Pluto on **July 1** and square to shocking Uranus on the **4th** could push you to a breaking point where you're ready to abandon your responsibilities. However, these aspects are meant to provoke a reassessment of your professional goals and family obligations. With a little patience and persistence, you can tap into unused resources and unmet desires that spur radically new approaches.

A subtle sense of order begins to take shape

in your life with structuring Saturn's forward turn and a loving Cancer New Moon in your 4th House on the **8th**. You may not see exactly where you're going yet, but a slow-rising tide of hope lifts your spirits. Fleet-footed Mercury's shift to direct motion on **July 20** helps you gather scattered thoughts and pull them together into a coherent vision. The Sun strides into bold Leo and your 5th House of Self-Expression on the **22nd**, just before the Full Moon in socially conscious Aquarius. Learning how to navigate from being a star (Leo) to being a valuable teammate (Aquarius) is the challenge and gift of this lunation.

KEEP IN MIND THIS MONTH

Think strategically; calibrating today's actions in terms of tomorrow's goals may seem less efficient now, but will pay big dividends later.

KEY DATES

★ **JULY 4-5**
velvet revolution
These are a couple of edgy days when your
impatience and a desire to do things your own
way could spark conflict. The Sun's harsh
square to independent Uranus on **July 4**
amplifies your hunger for freedom. You meet
even the slightest hint of authority with a
rebellious attitude and, perhaps, a desire to
flee. Yet on the **5th**, Mars forms an imaginative
quintile with Uranus that might give you the
liberty you need without creating a ruckus.
Trying unconventional approaches to problems
can help you avoid a crisis. Still, a delicate
semisquare between lovable Venus and
aggressive Mars reflects social awkwardness
or insecurity. If you can take criticism lightly
and without judging others, your vulnerability
will invite sweet connections instead of feelings
of rejection.

★ **JULY 12–13**

try a little tenderness

Mars's uncomfortable connection with the Moon's North Node on **July 12** can trigger irritable interactions with others. If you're feeling stressed or fatigued, it's best to put off serious discussions. Mars enters hesitant Cancer and your 4th House of Roots on the **13th**. You may be less available to the outer world while you attend to family matters and your own emotional needs. Your energy might not flow as freely since the spontaneity that allows you to act first and reflect later is frowned upon in this supersensitive sign.

SUPER NOVA DAYS

★ **JULY 20–22**

shoot for the stars

Mars's trines to stabilizing Saturn and altruistic Neptune on **July 20** create a beautiful blend of structure and imagination. You can be productive in an easygoing way that allows you to enjoy whatever tasks you undertake when Mars joins opportunistic Jupiter on the **22nd** to arouse ambitious dreams of travel and adventure. But if you're constrained from thinking big, or don't get the physical exercise you need, you could be steaming with anger or resentment. Venus's entry into detail-oriented Virgo and your 6th House of Service might bog you down in petty tasks. However, if you want to launch a new enterprise and reach the heights of success, you'll need to master all the small steps along the way.

★ **JULY 27**
let go to grow
It's better to do one thing with all your heart than to spread yourself too thin today. Mars's opposition to purging Pluto and the Sun's square to demanding Saturn reward you for your concentrated efforts. Your intense emotions could incite a heated battle; try to focus your passion on building something special, not tearing someone down.

AUGUST

TURN PLAY INTO PAY

You reach new heights of creativity with the Sun in dramatic Leo and your 5th House of Romance and Self-Expression until **August 22**. Remember, though, not to use this gift to play games when you could invest your energy in more important matters. The first of three powerful oppositions between enterprising Jupiter and transformational Pluto falls in your security-oriented 4th and 10th Houses on **August 7**. This can trigger a crisis at home or on the job that has you scrambling for safety—or, better, reviving an ambitious professional plan. This aspect recurs on **January 31** and **April 20, 2014**, providing two more chances to put these powerful planetary forces to practical use. The audacious Leo New Moon on the **6th** trines rebellious Uranus, triggering an urge for personal freedom and sparking originality. Communicative Mercury's move into your demonstrative 5th House on the **8th** makes your creative voice loud enough for everyone to hear.

Lovely Venus moves into relationship-oriented Libra and your 7th House of Partners on **August 16**, encouraging a sense of fair play in love and money. Keeping your allies on your side requires that you pay as much attention to their needs as your own. Your bright ideas may get your foot in the door, but without listening to others you won't be able to close the deal. The Aquarius Full Moon on the **20th** shines in your 11th House of Groups, challenging you to be a better friend and teammate. Learning how to adjust your methods of working is especially important with the Sun's move into modest Virgo and your 6th House of Service on **August 22**. Mental Mercury follows on the **23rd**, making this an excellent time to sharpen old skills and develop new ones.

KEEP IN MIND THIS MONTH

Getting attention is not the same as getting results. When you make a good impression, follow it up with hard work to maximize the return on your efforts.

KEY DATES

★ **AUGUST 1–2**
sweet and sour

Your restless spirit and natural resistance
to rules put you in a less-than-cooperative
mood. You're still resonating from yesterday's
explosive Mars-Uranus square, and now you
face a manipulative Sun-Pluto quincunx on
August 1 that can stir up power struggles.
Fortunately, Mars forms an efficient trine
with the Moon's North Node that guides you
to resolve relationship problems—as long as
your head doesn't get in the way of your heart.
In fact, you can be downright flirtatious on the
2nd, with a saucy little Venus-Mars sextile
adding delicious delight to your day.

★ **AUGUST 11**
changing currents

Your work habits may be a little loose with a
casual Mars-Neptune sesquisquare that's
better for noodling around than being efficient.
However, a sharp-eyed square between
analytical Mercury and exacting Saturn helps

you notice any errors and comment on them critically. Be perfectly clear with others about your intentions now to avoid hurt feelings later. Carefully choosing when to allow your mind to wander and when to concentrate inspires you to gracefully shift gears in response to these contrasting forces.

SUPER NOVA DAYS

★ **AUGUST 19-21**

embrace the unknown

On **August 19**, the occasionally arrogant Leo Sun in your outgoing 5th House clashes with a square between bombastic Jupiter and wayward Uranus on the **21st**. These aspects can provoke reckless behavior and self-aggrandizing statements that may be difficult to substantiate. The idealistic Aquarius Full Moon on the **20th** also inspires you to work for an important cause, but circumstances are too volatile to be sure that your belief is well founded. Open your mind and start gathering information instead of making any serious promises or commitments. Philosophical Jupiter squares radical Uranus again on

February 26 and **April 20, 2014**, in a long-lasting process that can drastically change your perspective. Determine whether your expectations have a realistic chance of success before putting all your eggs in one basket.

★ **AUGUST 27**
love without limits
Excess and self-indulgence entice you as your key planet, Mars, prances into your 5th House of Fun and Games while pleasure-loving Venus forms an unstable square with limitless Jupiter. You might overspend, oversell, or desire someone or something that costs a great deal more than it's worth. Stretching the boundaries of play and self-expression is fine as long as you don't push them beyond the breaking point.

SEPTEMBER

THE DEVIL'S IN THE DETAILS

Your success this month could hinge on your willingness to pay more attention to minor matters, even if they seem petty. The New Moon in precise Virgo occurs in your 6th House of Service on **September 5**, and you may feel picked on by overly critical people or stuck with boring tasks. But the New Moon's favorable sextile to benevolent Jupiter offers a world of opportunities if you become more conscientious about your work. Listening with an open mind becomes particularly valuable when verbal Mercury enters diplomatic Libra and your 7th House of Partners on the **9th**. Don't rush to respond to delicate questions; thinking through your answers lets you stand up for your side without alienating others. Relationship-conscious Venus's move into intense Scorpio and your 8th House of Deep Sharing on the **11th** is another signal to deal with people in a more thoughtful and considerate manner.

On **September 19**, the dreamy Pisces Full Moon in your 12th House of Secrets underscores the importance of discretion. You may want more time alone now, so make sure to monitor your energy levels and take breaks before you wear yourself out. Quiet communion with nature, contemplation of life's meaning, and other spiritual pursuits nourish your soul and enrich your inner world. You are able to accumulate professional power with subtlety and grace on the **21st** when ambitious Saturn makes its last sextile to generous Jupiter in a series that began on **December 26, 2012**, and repeated on **March 8**. The Sun's entry into cooperative Libra and your 7th House on **September 22** marks the Vernal Equinox, drawing creative, confident, and charming partners your way.

KEEP IN MIND THIS MONTH

If you feel hemmed in by a million and one little tasks, make each one a tiny work of art and you'll weave together a rich tapestry of fulfillment.

KEY DATES

★ **SEPTEMBER 2**
not so fast
A cranky, impulsive Mercury-Mars semisquare
can trigger thoughtless remarks that you may
immediately regret. When you feel the heat
of emotion rising, take a deep breath and
consider the consequences before speaking.
Mars's confusing quincunx with surreal
Neptune tends to turn you around in circles
instead of leading you where you want to go.
Don't just push harder out of frustration;
slowing down and rethinking your course is
more likely to get you back on track.

SUPER NOVA DAYS

★ **SEPTEMBER 9–11**
all or nothing
Patience, planning, and practice are needed
on **September 9**, when rambunctious Mars
in your 5th House of Play crosses paths in a
tense square to humorless Saturn in your 8th
House of Intimacy. No matter how entertaining
you are now, your audience may not be in a

responsive mood. Still, you can earn respect by working hard to complete one essential task—and gaining the trust of a demanding person may be worth the effort. The air is still thick on the **11th**, because a disturbing Mars-Pluto quincunx impedes your progress with power struggles. If you choose to engage in a battle and expect to win, be sure that you're ready to take it to the limit. However, you might suddenly realize that it's not worth the risk and wisely step aside.

★ **SEPTEMBER 14**
element of surprise
An inventive Mars-Uranus trine reveals new and unusual ways to deal with adversaries or tackle tough jobs. Brilliant originality empowers you to perform what may look like a miracle to worriers and doubters who expect you to fail.

★ **SEPTEMBER 17**
smooth operator
You are both clever and efficient today with a slick sextile between smart Mercury and

speedy Mars on your side. Your sharp thinking and fresh insights enable you to express yourself with good-natured humor, making your messages easy to understand and delightful to hear.

★ **SEPTEMBER 26-28**
opposites attract
The Sun forms an irritating semisquare to impatient Mars on **September 26**, stirring up trouble. You can, however, consciously apply this high-octane energy with a soft touch that works to your advantage. Try standing up for yourself with a smile, or gently pushing with a positive attitude. A sexy Venus-Mars square on the **28th** blurs the line between flirting and fighting, making it nearly impossible to know where you stand with someone. It's natural to have mixed feelings that might provoke irrational behavior, but avoid going too far and too fast too soon.

OCTOBER

THE PERILS AND PLEASURES OF PARTNERSHIP

Fasten your seat belt, because a wild New Moon in your 7th House of Partners on **October 4** can take you and your relationships on a roller-coaster ride. A Sun-Moon conjunction in lovely Libra is normally associated with making sweet alliances and comfortable new connections. This lunation, however, opposes disruptive Uranus and squares provocative Pluto, which can incite power struggles and sudden shifts of circumstances and moods. Remaining reasonable when you deal with emotionally inconsistent people and calming your own volcanic feelings can make the difference between war and peace now. You're tempted to run from demanding unions on the **7th** when romantic Venus enters carefree Sagittarius and your 9th House of Faraway Places. Pursuing interests in travel, higher learning, and people from different cultures will be rewarding as long as you're not using them to escape your current reality.

Once your ruling planet, Mars, moves into precise Virgo and your 6th House of Work on

October 15, focus on refining old methods and applying your creativity in practical ways. If you're bored by your job, investing energy in a hobby or developing a new skill should perk you up. The independent Aries Full Moon on the **18th** lands in your 1st House of Personality as a reminder to address your own needs before worrying about others. The happier you are now, the more valuable you'll be to those around you. On **October 21**, rational Mercury's retrograde turn in your 8th House of Intimacy reminds you to back up and renegotiate your relationships. The Sun's shift into intuitive Scorpio and your 8th House on the **23rd** attracts strong partners and shows how teaming up with the right people will add power and passion to your life.

KEEP IN MIND THIS MONTH

Expressing what you want from others is the essential first step to clearing the air and getting the most out of your alliances.

KEY DATES

★ **OCTOBER 2**
fixer-upper
A clever quintile between inquisitive Mercury
and enterprising Mars reveals shortcuts
and inspires creative problem-solving ideas.
Now is the perfect time for untangling
misunderstandings related to money and love.
If you feel stuck in an unhappy situation, look
a bit deeper—you'll probably find a surprising
solution.

SUPER NOVA DAYS

★ **OCTOBER 4–7**
taking it up a notch
If you feel suffocated by any external pressure
right now, it's because Mars's strange
sesquisquares to suspicious Pluto on **October 5**
and nervous Uranus on the **7th** indicate serious
irritations. These hard aspects with astrology's
two most disruptive planets on the heels of
the ambiguous Libra New Moon on the **4th**
can intensify complex relationship issues.
You're ready to push back with anger—which

is understandable, but it's also more likely to aggravate the tension than resolve it. If you can instead apply these kinetic forces with conscious intent and originality, you could get out of a rut and create exciting new avenues of personal and professional expression.

★ **OCTOBER 19**
sweet surrender
Today your ruling planet, hard-charging Mars, opposes spacey Neptune. It's a slippery aspect that can lead you astray, tricking you into chasing illusions or working with unreliable individuals. Demonstrating a tender touch, acting with compassion, following your intuition, and engaging in metaphysical activities are all ways to stay on your spiritual path.

★ **OCTOBER 24**
larger than life
You're tempted to take on more than you can handle or promise more than you can deliver with active Mars's inelegant semisquare to exuberant Jupiter. There's nothing wrong

with high aspirations, but your tendency to go too far or too fast won't help you reach your goals. If you're overflowing with energy, full of self-righteousness, or fed up and ready to fight, think carefully before firing the first shot. Retrograde Mercury's smart quintile with Mars is excellent for reviewing your current plans and tying up loose ends.

★ **OCTOBER 31**
keep your eyes on the prize
Establish well-defined priorities and you'll have a highly productive day. A powerful Mars-Pluto trine is your sword for cutting through clutter, eliminating obstacles, and acting with quiet authority. You can finally complete unfinished business you've been avoiding. Don't lose sight of your primary objectives—a quirky Mars-Uranus quincunx is liable to interrupt you with unexpected distractions.

NOVEMBER

RELATIONSHIP REALIGNMENT

There are rumbles of change bubbling below
the surface that could break through and alter
the nature of an important partnership this
month. November starts with the fourth of seven
transformational squares between Uranus and
Pluto on the **1st** that ratchets up tension between
your need for independence and the heavy hand
of authority that's thwarting your progress.
On the **3rd**, a Solar Eclipse in power-sensitive
Scorpio joins sobering Saturn in your 8th House
of Intimacy, which forces you to make a tough
decision. You can commit to work harder to keep a
valuable alliance afloat—or recognize that you're
not going to get what you want from it. Either way,
it's better to make a choice than have one imposed
upon you. Philosophical Jupiter's retrograde turn
in your 4th House of Roots on **November 7** invites
reflection as you look back to the past and reorient
your plans for the future.

On **November 10**, mobile Mercury begins
moving forward again in your 8th House to
facilitate communication in critical collaborations.
Think carefully before you speak or react to what

others say since words have more impact than usual now. On the **17th**, the sensible Taurus Full Moon falls in your 2nd House of Self-Worth, spurring moneymaking ideas and encouraging resourceful behavior. The Sun shoots into visionary Sagittarius and your 9th House of Travel and Higher Education on the **21st**, lifting your focus above the normal fray of daily life to visualize a more expansive future. Aiming higher infuses you with hope, but the Sun's stressful square with nebulous Neptune on the **24th** could carry you beyond the bounds of reason.

KEEP IN MIND THIS MONTH

Don't settle for less from the key people in your life. Define your needs and ask for what you want if you hope to be rewarded with greater returns.

KEY DATES

SUPER NOVA DAYS

★ **NOVEMBER 1–3**

nothing ventured, nothing gained

An alert sextile between curious Mercury and capable Mars on **November 1** can guide you through the rapids of intense emotions that are churning now. The creative consciousness of the Sun's sextile to Mars on the **3rd** helps you stay on course during the day's complicated New Moon Eclipse in passionate Scorpio. In fact, you might even be able to turn a loss into a gain if you are persistent, persuasive, and know exactly what you want. It's understandable if frustration drives you to think about going it alone, but the challenge of working with a demanding colleague pays off if you don't give up.

★ **NOVEMBER 9**

efficiency expert

This is a very productive day, for a hardworking Mars-Saturn sextile provides you with a perfect balance of effort and discipline. You can assess a task and complete it without wasting a single move. Make the time to sharpen your skills, especially when you have an experienced teacher to show you the ropes.

★ NOVEMBER 14–15
on-the-job jitters

Expect the unexpected on **November 14–15**, when valuable Venus in your 10th House of Career forms hard aspects. You may experience upsets at work when an unpredictable square with Uranus brings surprises, and resentment may be evoked as Venus conjuncts punishing Pluto. But if you're willing to be flexible and handle awkward individuals and unexpected situations, you could earn new respect. On the other hand, boredom or unfair working conditions might provoke you to think about changing your place of employment.

★ NOVEMBER 19
lean on me

Competent Mars in your 6th House of Skills cruises into a cool sextile with optimistic Jupiter, showcasing your ability to manage

complex tasks with an easygoing attitude.
Even if you're so busy that you feel pulled in
several directions, you know how to prioritize
your time and set a good example for others.
If co-workers or customers are nervous and
insecure, your calm steadiness under pressure
can reduce everyone's stress.

★ **NOVEMBER 29**
in it to win it
The confident Sun in upbeat Sagittarius
sometimes leads you to promise more than you
can deliver or raises your own expectations too
high. But today's creative solar quintile to Mars
in practical Virgo gives you the tools to expand
your reach while keeping your feet firmly on
the ground. If you have an idea to pitch, a
product to sell, or a job you want, this dynamic
Sun-Mars connection shows others that your
high level of enthusiasm is rooted in a deep
commitment and reinforced by your capability
to justify it.

DECEMBER

OVER THE RAINBOW

You are drawn toward extreme adventure this month; distant places and mind-expanding activities are calling you to fly far away. On **December 2**, the restless Sagittarius New Moon falls in your 9th House of Big Ideas, arousing the desire to widen your horizons. Metaphysical Neptune's square to this lunation taps into a spiritual yearning or, less desirably, pulls you toward unrealistic fantasies that are likely to remain out of reach. Innovative Uranus, though, forms a favorable trine to this Sun-Moon conjunction, creating unexpected opportunities for travel and learning. This is perfect timing since intellectual Mercury launches into cavalier Sagittarius on the **4th** to open your mind and inspire bolder speech. Your ruling planet, Mars, enters diplomatic Libra and your 7th House of Partners on **December 7**, an excellent time for initiating new connections, taking a current relationship to a higher level, or going public with an important project. Still, be sure to tread lightly and listen to the feedback you receive rather than plunging ahead impulsively.

ARIES 2013

The Full Moon in versatile Gemini on
December 17 kicks up communication in your
3rd House of Data Collection. Chatting with
others is useful for gathering information,
especially when it comes to filling in the blanks
where you have big ideas but lack some key data.
The Winter Solstice is marked by the Sun's entry
into responsible Capricorn and your 10th House
of Career on the **21st**, boosting your ambition
and increasing your public responsibilities.
Amicable Venus, also in the 10th House, turns
retrograde later in the day, reminding you to
repair professional relationships and perhaps
reconnect with old colleagues. Mercury moves
into your 10th House on the **24th**, challenging you
to clear your mind and get busy organizing work-
related projects.

KEEP IN MIND THIS MONTH

*It's easy to find the motivation and discipline to
persevere through thick and thin when you are
reaching for a goal that passionately inspires you.*

KEY DATES

★ **DECEMBER 3**

sharp as a tack

Mercury in discerning Scorpio and your
8th House of Deep Sharing sextiles Mars
in your practical 6th House of Habits,
clarifying your thinking and adding powerful
impact to your message. Today you're a more
critical listener who quickly understands
which information will be most useful and
which to ignore. You'll find it easier now to
nudge an ally in any direction you want her or
him to go.

★ **DECEMBER 9**

give peace a chance

You're able to stand up for yourself today in a
pleasant, nonthreatening manner when Mars
in gracious Libra forms a creative quintile with
opinionated Jupiter in self-protective Cancer. If
you're avoiding a confrontation because you're
worried about starting a fight, this transit
provides the finesse to make your points and
gain the support of someone who might have

been your adversary, but is now more likely to become your friend.

★ **DECEMBER 13–15**
stay on the straight and narrow
You struggle to maintain your equilibrium with others when Mars slips on a banana peel of a quincunx to woozy Neptune on **December 13**. You might be able to work around a problem, but you're equally likely to waste time with distractions or avoidance techniques. If you happen to wander off course, a stressful aspect from exigent Saturn to Mars on the **14th** holds you accountable. However, your willingness to pay attention to external signals can work wonders on the **15th** thanks to the efficiency of an intelligent Mercury-Mars quintile.

★ **DECEMBER 25**
independence day
Expect an explosive holiday with an electrifying Mars-Uranus opposition ready to unleash surprises and undercut cooperation. Your nervous energy and impatience could

accumulate and mar your judgment, perhaps even leading to an argument or accident. But instead of acting rashly or rebelling against old rules and traditions just to be contrary, seek a fresh way to celebrate that captures the brilliance of this dynamic aspect in a positive manner.

SUPER NOVA DAYS

★ **DECEMBER 30–31**

yell fire!

The year ends with a bang as an anti-authoritarian Sun-Uranus square and a ruthless Mars-Pluto square ignite rebellious feelings on **December 30**. It might not take much to push your buttons; powerful emotions have already been growing and are ripe for expression. Mouthy Mercury enters the picture on the **31st** with a conjunction to potent Pluto and a provocative square to combative Mars that could produce angry words. Taming your temper and saying what's on your mind with as much self-restraint as possible could avoid an end-of-the-year meltdown.

APPENDIXES

★

2013 MONTH-AT-A-GLANCE ASTROCALENDAR

★

FAMOUS ARIES

★

ARIES IN LOVE

TUESDAY 1	
WEDNESDAY 2	
THURSDAY 3	
FRIDAY 4 ★	Remain sensitive to the needs of your audience
SATURDAY 5	
SUNDAY 6	
MONDAY 7 ★	**SUPER NOVA DAY** Follow a well-defined plan
TUESDAY 8	
WEDNESDAY 9	
THURSDAY 10	
FRIDAY 11 ●	
SATURDAY 12	
SUNDAY 13	
MONDAY 14 ★	Develop a neglected talent or an under-utilized skill
TUESDAY 15 ★	
WEDNESDAY 16 ★	
THURSDAY 17	
FRIDAY 18	
SATURDAY 19	
SUNDAY 20 ★	Reckless behavior and sudden anger can undercut trust
MONDAY 21	
TUESDAY 22	
WEDNESDAY 23	
THURSDAY 24	
FRIDAY 25	
SATURDAY 26 ★	O Temper your reactions with self-restraint
SUNDAY 27	
MONDAY 28	
TUESDAY 29	
WEDNESDAY 30	
THURSDAY 31	

★ designates key date

FRIDAY 1

SATURDAY 2

SUNDAY 3

MONDAY 4 ★ Taking the scenic route might save you time and energy

TUESDAY 5

WEDNESDAY 6

THURSDAY 7

FRIDAY 8 ★ **SUPER NOVA DAYS** Take a moment to organize your thoughts

SATURDAY 9 ★

SUNDAY 10 ★ ●

MONDAY 11

TUESDAY 12

WEDNESDAY 13

THURSDAY 14

FRIDAY 15 ★ You are working with a higher level of efficiency now

SATURDAY 16 ★

SUNDAY 17

MONDAY 18

TUESDAY 19

WEDNESDAY 20

THURSDAY 21

FRIDAY 22

SATURDAY 23

SUNDAY 24

MONDAY 25 ★ ○ Repair damage and restore trust

TUESDAY 26 ★

WEDNESDAY 27

THURSDAY 28

FRIDAY 1	
SATURDAY 2	
SUNDAY 3 ★	Cut through complexity to get to the core of the matter

MONDAY 4	
TUESDAY 5	
WEDNESDAY 6	
THURSDAY 7 ★	Approach the situation from a totally different angle

FRIDAY 8	
SATURDAY 9	
SUNDAY 10	
MONDAY 11 ★ ●	Be proactive in pursuing your goals

TUESDAY 12 ★	
WEDNESDAY 13	
THURSDAY 14	
FRIDAY 15	
SATURDAY 16	
SUNDAY 17	
MONDAY 18	
TUESDAY 19	
WEDNESDAY 20 ★ **SUPER NOVA DAYS** Rebellion could spark impulsive behavior	

THURSDAY 21 ★	
FRIDAY 22 ★	
SATURDAY 23	
SUNDAY 24	
MONDAY 25 ★	Concentrate on one task at a time

TUESDAY 26 ★	
WEDNESDAY 27 ★ ○	
THURSDAY 28 ★	
FRIDAY 29	
SATURDAY 30	
SUNDAY 31	

MONDAY 1 ★ Connect with positive people who encourage your growth

TUESDAY 2

WEDNESDAY 3

THURSDAY 4

FRIDAY 5

SATURDAY 6 ★ Indulge in the beauty of nature and art now

SUNDAY 7 ★

MONDAY 8

TUESDAY 9

WEDNESDAY 10 ●

THURSDAY 11

FRIDAY 12

SATURDAY 13 ★ Do your research before making important statements

SUNDAY 14

MONDAY 15

TUESDAY 16

WEDNESDAY 17 ★ SUPER NOVA DAY Your temper could get the best of you

THURSDAY 18

FRIDAY 19

SATURDAY 20

SUNDAY 21

MONDAY 22

TUESDAY 23

WEDNESDAY 24

THURSDAY 25 ○

FRIDAY 26 ★ Tune into your environment

SATURDAY 27

SUNDAY 28

MONDAY 29

TUESDAY 30

WEDNESDAY 1 ★ Stick to a plan and don't wander off track

THURSDAY 2

FRIDAY 3

SATURDAY 4

SUNDAY 5 ★ **SUPER NOVA DAYS** Don't take no for an answer now

---

MONDAY 6 ★

TUESDAY 7 ★

WEDNESDAY 8

THURSDAY 9 ●

FRIDAY 10

SATURDAY 11

SUNDAY 12

MONDAY 13 ★ Emotions could overcome reason today

TUESDAY 14

WEDNESDAY 15

THURSDAY 16

FRIDAY 17

SATURDAY 18

SUNDAY 19

MONDAY 20 ★ Avoid making rash decisions

TUESDAY 21

WEDNESDAY 22

THURSDAY 23

FRIDAY 24

SATURDAY 25 ★ ○ Adapt swiftly to suddenly changing circumstances

---

SUNDAY 26 ★

MONDAY 27

TUESDAY 28

WEDNESDAY 29

THURSDAY 30

FRIDAY 31

SATURDAY 1	
SUNDAY 2	
MONDAY 3	
TUESDAY 4	
WEDNESDAY 5	
THURSDAY 6	
FRIDAY 7 ★	**SUPER NOVA DAYS** Adjust your methods and expectations

SATURDAY 8 ★ ●	
SUNDAY 9	
MONDAY 10	
TUESDAY 11	
WEDNESDAY 12	
THURSDAY 13	
FRIDAY 14	
SATURDAY 15 ★	Clean up clutter and finish off minor tasks

SUNDAY 16 ★	
MONDAY 17 ★	
TUESDAY 18	
WEDNESDAY 19 ★	Discuss personal matters with care and tenderness

THURSDAY 20 ★	
FRIDAY 21 ★	
SATURDAY 22	
SUNDAY 23 ○	
MONDAY 24	
TUESDAY 25	
WEDNESDAY 26	
THURSDAY 27 ★	Recognize the limits of others

FRIDAY 28 ★	
SATURDAY 29	
SUNDAY 30	

MONDAY 1	
TUESDAY 2	
WEDNESDAY 3	
THURSDAY 4 ★	Take criticism lightly

FRIDAY 5 ★	
SATURDAY 6	
SUNDAY 7	
MONDAY 8 ●	
TUESDAY 9	
WEDNESDAY 10	
THURSDAY 11	
FRIDAY 12 ★	Put off a serious discussion until you're ready

SATURDAY 13 ★	
SUNDAY 14	
MONDAY 15	
TUESDAY 16	
WEDNESDAY 17	
THURSDAY 18	
FRIDAY 19	
SATURDAY 20 ★	**SUPER NOVA DAYS** Create a mix of structure and imagination

SUNDAY 21 ★	
MONDAY 22 ★ ○	
TUESDAY 23	
WEDNESDAY 24	
THURSDAY 25	
FRIDAY 26	
SATURDAY 27 ★	Put your passion into building something special

SUNDAY 28	
MONDAY 29	
TUESDAY 30	
WEDNESDAY 31	

THURSDAY 1 ★ Resolve relationship problems

FRIDAY 2 ★

SATURDAY 3

SUNDAY 4

MONDAY 5

TUESDAY 6 ●

WEDNESDAY 7

THURSDAY 8

FRIDAY 9

SATURDAY 10

SUNDAY 11 ★ Be perfectly clear about your intentions

MONDAY 12

TUESDAY 13

WEDNESDAY 14

THURSDAY 15

FRIDAY 16

SATURDAY 17

SUNDAY 18

MONDAY 19 ★ SUPER NOVA DAYS Work for an important cause

TUESDAY 20 ★ ○

WEDNESDAY 21 ★

THURSDAY 22

FRIDAY 23

SATURDAY 24

SUNDAY 25

MONDAY 26

TUESDAY 27 ★ Stretch the boundaries of play and self-expression

WEDNESDAY 28

THURSDAY 29

FRIDAY 30

SATURDAY 31

SUNDAY 1

MONDAY 2 ★ Slow down and rethink your course of action

TUESDAY 3

WEDNESDAY 4

THURSDAY 5 ●

FRIDAY 6

SATURDAY 7

SUNDAY 8

MONDAY 9 ★ SUPER NOVA DAYS Earn respect by working diligently

TUESDAY 10 ★

WEDNESDAY 11 ★

THURSDAY 12

FRIDAY 13

SATURDAY 14 ★ Tackle tough jobs in new ways

SUNDAY 15

MONDAY 16

TUESDAY 17 ★ Express yourself with good-natured humor

WEDNESDAY 18

THURSDAY 19 ○

FRIDAY 20

SATURDAY 21

SUNDAY 22

MONDAY 23

TUESDAY 24

WEDNESDAY 25

THURSDAY 26 ★ Stand up for yourself with a smile

FRIDAY 27 ★

SATURDAY 28 ★

SUNDAY 29

MONDAY 30

TUESDAY 1

WEDNESDAY 2 ★ Untangle misunderstandings related to money and love

THURSDAY 3

FRIDAY 4 ★ ● SUPER NOVA DAYS Resentment arises quickly

SATURDAY 5 ★

SUNDAY 6 ★

MONDAY 7 ★

TUESDAY 8

WEDNESDAY 9

THURSDAY 10

FRIDAY 11

SATURDAY 12

SUNDAY 13

MONDAY 14

TUESDAY 15

WEDNESDAY 16

THURSDAY 17

FRIDAY 18 ○

SATURDAY 19 ★ Stop struggling so hard

SUNDAY 20

MONDAY 21

TUESDAY 22

WEDNESDAY 23

THURSDAY 24 ★ Review your current plans and tie up loose ends

FRIDAY 25

SATURDAY 26

SUNDAY 27

MONDAY 28

TUESDAY 29

WEDNESDAY 30

THURSDAY 31 ★ Establish well-defined priorities

FRIDAY 1 ★ **SUPER NOVA DAYS** Turn a loss into a gain

SATURDAY 2 ★

SUNDAY 3 ★ ●

MONDAY 4

TUESDAY 5

WEDNESDAY 6

THURSDAY 7

FRIDAY 8

SATURDAY 9 ★ Make the time to sharpen your skills

SUNDAY 10

MONDAY 11

TUESDAY 12

WEDNESDAY 13

THURSDAY 14 ★ Expect the unexpected

FRIDAY 15 ★

SATURDAY 16

SUNDAY 17 ○

MONDAY 18

TUESDAY 19 ★ Set a good example for others

WEDNESDAY 20

THURSDAY 21

FRIDAY 22

SATURDAY 23

SUNDAY 24

MONDAY 25

TUESDAY 26

WEDNESDAY 27

THURSDAY 28

FRIDAY 29 ★ Expand your reach while keeping your feet on the ground

---

SATURDAY 30

SUNDAY 1	
MONDAY 2	●
TUESDAY 3	★ Clarify your thinking

WEDNESDAY 4	
THURSDAY 5	
FRIDAY 6	
SATURDAY 7	
SUNDAY 8	
MONDAY 9	★ Give peace a chance

TUESDAY 10	
WEDNESDAY 11	
THURSDAY 12	
FRIDAY 13	★ Maintaining your equilibrium may not be easy

SATURDAY 14	★
SUNDAY 15	★
MONDAY 16	
TUESDAY 17	○
WEDNESDAY 18	
THURSDAY 19	
FRIDAY 20	
SATURDAY 21	
SUNDAY 22	
MONDAY 23	
TUESDAY 24	
WEDNESDAY 25	★ Seek a fresh way to celebrate

THURSDAY 26	
FRIDAY 27	
SATURDAY 28	
SUNDAY 29	
MONDAY 30	★ **SUPER NOVA DAYS** Tame your temper

TUESDAY 31	★

FAMOUS ARIES

Johann Sebastian Bach	★	3/21/1685
Rosie O'Donnell	★	3/21/1962
Clyde Barrow	★	3/21/1909
Stephen Sondheim	★	3/22/1930
William Shatner	★	3/22/1931
Andrew Lloyd Webber	★	3/22/1948
Bob Costas	★	3/22/1952
Reese Witherspoon	★	3/22/1976
Chico Marx	★	3/22/1887
Chaka Khan	★	3/23/1953
Tommy Hilfiger	★	3/24/1951
Joan Crawford	★	3/24/1904
Peyton Manning	★	3/24/1976
Steve McQueen	★	3/24/1930
Harry Houdini	★	3/24/1874
Aretha Franklin	★	3/25/1942
Elton John	★	3/25/1947
Sarah Jessica Parker	★	3/25/1965
Howard Cosell	★	3/25/1920
Gloria Steinem	★	3/25/1934
Sheryl Swoopes	★	3/25/1971
Flannery O'Connor	★	3/25/1925
Diana Ross	★	3/26/1944
Robert Frost	★	3/26/1874
Sandra Day O'Connor	★	3/26/1930
Leonard Nimoy	★	3/26/1931
Bob Woodward	★	3/26/1943
Quentin Tarantino	★	3/27/1963
Mariah Carey	★	3/27/1970
Reba McEntire	★	3/28/1955
Cy Young	★	3/29/1867
Warren Beatty	★	3/30/1937
Eric Clapton	★	3/30/1945
Vincent van Gogh	★	3/30/1853
Celine Dion	★	3/30/1968
Christopher Walken	★	3/31/1943
Al Gore	★	3/31/1948

FAMOUS ARIES

Debbie Reynolds	★	4/1/1932
Hans Christian Andersen	★	4/2/1805
Marvin Gaye	★	4/2/1939
Marlon Brando	★	4/3/1924
Jane Goodall	★	4/3/1934
Wayne Newton	★	4/3/1942
Doris Day	★	4/3/1924
Eddie Murphy	★	4/3/1961
Maya Angelou	★	4/4/1928
Bette Davis	★	4/5/1908
Colin Powell	★	4/5/1937
Gregory Peck	★	4/5/1916
Booker T. Washington	★	4/5/1856
Butch Cassidy	★	4/6/1866
Francis Ford Coppola	★	4/7/1939
Jackie Chan	★	4/7/1954
Billie Holiday	★	4/7/1915
Russell Crowe	★	4/7/1964
Joseph Pulitzer	★	4/10/1847
Ethel Kennedy	★	4/11/1928
Tom Clancy	★	4/12/1947
David Letterman	★	4/12/1947
David Cassidy	★	4/12/1950
Samuel Beckett	★	4/13/1906
Thomas Jefferson	★	4/13/1743
Loretta Lynn	★	4/14/1935
Leonardo da Vinci	★	4/15/1452
Bessie Smith	★	4/15/1894
Charlie Chaplin	★	4/16/1889
Dusty Springfield	★	4/16/1939
Nikita Khrushchev	★	4/17/1894
Thornton Wilder	★	4/17/1897
Clarence Darrow	★	4/18/1857
Conan O'Brien	★	4/18/1963
Kate Hudson	★	4/19/1979

ARIES IN LOVE

ARIES & ARIES (MARCH 21–APRIL 19)

You Rams are fiery, impulsive, and pioneering, and you love romance—especially new ones. With another Aries, you find yourself in a very dynamic relationship that has a constant competitive edge. You'll each need to watch for potential flare-ups and ego clashes. Since it takes two to tango, why not learn to be patient and levelheaded with each other? This will help to smooth out the rough spots between you two strongwilled individuals. With another Aries, you can certainly blaze a trail of flaming passion and zest as long as each of you remains patient with the other. Try not to make too many long-term plans, for if you don't become bored with the relationship, then your partner might. It will take influences from other stabilizing planets, like Saturn, to give your relationship staying power. Without additional planetary anchors, you have a reputation for leaving a string of unfinished business behind. At least this is a relationship where you can live in the present and be happy.

ARIES & TAURUS (APRIL 20–MAY 20)

Your enthusiasm can help to perk up the sometimes mellow Taurus. You Aries are ruled by fiery Mars and tend to be more restless than your Taurus partner, who is ruled by the love planet, Venus. It may be necessary for you to take the lead in many activities. On the other hand, your bullheaded Taurus amour is more persevering than you'll ever be and will likely bring tenacity and endurance to the relationship. You are the hotheaded and impulsive one, but the Moon in an earth sign (Taurus, Virgo, or Capricorn) or water sign (Cancer, Scorpio, or Pisces) in your chart may mellow you out. Your mate may not often lose his or her temper, but when it does happen, you had better watch out! Both of you can be reactionary and somewhat childlike in your response to authority and leadership. When it comes to play, however, the two of you can romp and roam through the fields of life. Slow down, Aries, and you'll be able to enjoy this relationship for a long time to come.

ARIES & GEMINI (MAY 21–JUNE 20)

Your fire burns brighter when in the company of an airy Gemini, and you can make quite a compatible couple. You're both eager and alive with plenty of ambition, vision, and verve. Because of your impulsive spontaneity, however, trouble exists when you decide to veer off in search of new and exciting potentials. Just when the search becomes boring and you decide to return to the relationship, your curious and clever Gemini friend announces he or she has found an interest in the greener pastures of life. So the biggest problem you might have in partnering with a Gemini is that while you're busy distracting yourself outside the relationship, they won't be sitting home waiting for your return. Without supporting contacts between the weightier outer planets in your charts, this relationship may never have time to mature. On the other hand, if you keep your Gemini partner fully engaged, they will not lose interest. You'll need to learn how to be more tolerant before you can fully settle in for the long haul of long-term commitment. Even if your relationship doesn't last forever, chances are that it will bring you much fun and excitement.

ARIES & CANCER (JUNE 21–JULY 22)

You Aries folks have fiery Mars as your key or ruling planet. As such, you aren't eager to show your emotions. In fact, you take care of things by acting rather than talking about your feelings. You're candid, spontaneous, and quick to recover from emotional setbacks. This is so different from your Cancer partner, who is ruled by the watery Moon. Cancers are deeply emotional, caring, and sensitive. A tendency to nurture and protect their own feelings can cause them to withdraw from the lighthearted whims that you Aries find so enjoyable. Cancers may cramp your style, for they seem to worry about everything, while you'd rather do it now and worry about it later—if ever. It's not all bleak, though. A good relationship is possible if you can learn to honor the sincere emotions of your Cancer friend, but in turn, he or she must learn to respect your need to act spontaneously. If Venus in your chart is in Pisces or Taurus, you will be better equipped to appreciate your lover. If your Moon is in a water sign, chances for compatibility are increased. Either way, this can be a dynamic relationship that pushes each of you into new ways of expressing your love.

ARIES & LEO (JULY 23–AUGUST 22)

Fire signs tend to work well with other fire signs, so this can be a good and lasting pair as long as there is plenty of excitement, romance, and play. Both of you love a good time and will put sports, adventure, and parties on top of your priority list. You are impulsively active by nature and may be inspired by your creative, expressive, and fun-loving Leo partner. You are more likely to follow a whim, and it will take a very secure Leo to trust you enough to give you the freedom you'll want. Meanwhile, your Lion is loyal and faithful, as long as he or she feels loved or even adored. You both love to be the center of attention and would never turn your backs on an opportunity to be admired. There is no shortage of physical passion here, especially as a way to burn off excess anger. If, however, the Moon in your chart is in Taurus, Scorpio, or Aquarius, compatibility may be more difficult to achieve. It would be a good idea for you two limelight lovers to admire each other, express your love actively, and avoid excessive competition. Long-term potentials include an active and joyous life of laughter, entertainment, and love.

ARIES & VIRGO (AUGUST 23–SEPT. 22)

Your spontaneous and childlike ways can be critically and harshly judged by analytical Virgo. Virgos are drawn toward service and hard work and make wonderful hosts or hostesses. They're usually first to tidy up after a party. You, on the other hand, may on occasion forget the golden rule of service, preferring the gaiety of social pleasure and the personal gratification of the moment. Good humor is a key that can unlock the potential success between such different styles— your impulsiveness and Virgo's compulsiveness. Virgos can have tremendous wit, and you Aries really know how to laugh at yourself. If your Moon is in an earth sign (Taurus, Virgo, or Capricorn), your chances for long-term compatibility are increased, since your styles may not be as different as described. If you can each manage to respect your natural differences and make adjustments to your lifestyle, you can create a long-lasting team with a Virgo partner. Your open and cheerful ways can keep your Virgo happy, while they bring a level of mental clarity into your life that can really help you along on your path.

ARIES & LIBRA (SEPT. 23–OCT. 22)

Libra is the sign that is exactly opposite you in
the zodiac, and as the old saying goes, opposites
attract. You are like opposite sides of the same
coin, but of course, this means that you share the
same coin. You are naturally more interested in
personal matters of the ego. Your Libra partner
is probably more curious about what others think
and do. You operate in terms of self-motivating
desires while your partner gains self-knowledge
through other people's experiences and ideas.
As you Aries tend to be quite independent, your
Libra is wired for relationships and loves to relate
to others. Together you balance each other and
tend to blend well. If the Moon or Mars in your
chart is in an air sign (Gemini, Libra, or Aquarius),
compatibility will be easier as you better relate
to the intellectual aspects of your lover. No
matter what the other planets add into the mix,
your involvement with a Libra can teach you the
virtue of relationships, valuable people skills, and
flexibility.

ARIES & SCORPIO (OCT. 23–NOV. 21)

You Aries can burn on the hot side, and with a Scorpio you may have met your match. Passion is the common thread that intertwines you in this relationship. Your Scorpio partner's fire is deep, relentless, and consuming. Meanwhile, your fire blazes brightly with sheer excitement and then tends to settle down as you recharge your batteries. Can your emotional and moody Scorpio mate keep up with your outward expression of enthusiasm and joy? Perhaps. But you'll have to learn the virtue of solid commitment and understand the fact that you are in it for the long haul. If Venus in your chart is in Pisces, you will better appreciate the feeling dimensions of your Scorpio lover. In fact, compatibility is enhanced if your Moon is in any water sign (Cancer, Scorpio, or Pisces). You can teach your Scorpio how to have a more lighthearted attitude toward life. He or she can put you in touch with the power of your own passion. Together, you are intense and focused, and will need plenty of time to explore the mysterious and pleasurable realms of love.

ARIES & SAGITTARIUS (NOV. 22–DEC. 21)

You are quite the dynamic duo. Even when you're on your own, you are usually ready to do something new and exciting. Now, with a Sagittarius, you make an action-oriented pair, for you love to be on the go almost as much as your Sagittarius does. Your impulsive temperament and quick-to-change ways may challenge the Sagittarius who prefers to set goals and strives to accomplish the tasks. Other planets in your chart, such as the Moon or Mars in an earth sign, may slow you down or make you less impulsive, thus increasing compatibility. Nevertheless, when you are with another fire sign, you stimulate each other toward new heights of accomplishment and achievement. Sagittarius's optimistic character is compatible with your cheerful disposition. With a Sagittarius, you adrenaline-seeking Aries will seldom find yourself caught in a rut of boring routines. Together you will blaze trails, light the fires of excitement, and create adventures with each other.

ARIES & CAPRICORN (DEC. 22–JAN. 19)

Quick and eager for excitement, you hit solid ground (or maybe a wall) with the practical purposefulness of a Saturnine Capricorn. You Rams butt heads with Capricorn the Goat, unless you can find a way to respect and honor each other's personal goals and drives. You may be great at starting things but are less accomplished at seeing them through. Of course, the specific placement of the planets at your birth may alter this. For example, with Venus in Taurus, you may be more attracted to the practical side of your Capricorn lover. With the Moon or Mars in any earth sign or water sign, chances for long-term compatibility are increased. Regardless, when you are with a result-oriented Capricorn, you're going to have to learn to complete the tasks you start in order to win your partner's trust, while your Capricorn mate needs to learn how to be comfortable moving with your occasional impulsive needs for change. You're going to have to get used to your partner taking on more responsibilities than you would. You can help cheer your mate up with your enthusiastic encouragement when he or she is overwhelmed.

ARIES & AQUARIUS (JAN. 20–FEB. 18)

You pioneering Aries get along famously with inventive and progressive Aquarius as long as the know-it-all tendency of the Aquarius doesn't ignite your hotheadedness into an argument. You need plenty of room for independence, and the good news is that airy Aquarius needs enough emotional detachment that you'll be able to have the freedom you need within this relationship. Both of you enjoy new beginnings, the excitement of starting over, and enthusiastically sharing your dreams with each other. There is rarely a dull moment in this relationship, unless there are other planetary indicators in your charts, such as Venus, Mars, or the Moon in any earth sign (Taurus, Virgo, or Capricorn). The question between you two might be: "Who is going to become the more stable one?" Both of you can be surefooted, courageous, and mentally equipped to take on the world. With purpose and determination, the two of you could uplift those around you with new perspectives and opinions about life.

ARIES & PISCES (FEB. 19–MARCH 20)

As the first sign of the zodiac, you Aries are very different than Pisces, which is the last sign. You're robust, aggressive, and outgoing. Meanwhile, Pisces is sensitive, intuitive, and introverted.

You will, however, probably love the imaginative impulse of your Pisces partner, who will enjoy your ability to enhance their dreams by taking actions to make them real. The problem is that your raw and natural instincts, if unchecked, can sometimes overwhelm Pisces's refined personality. Lucky for you, Pisces can be compassionate and understanding. As long as your actions are pure and well intended, Pisces will try to find a way to remain flexible, supportive, and receptive to your sheer enthusiasm. Sometimes, depending on other planetary placements in your birth chart, you Aries may have Piscean influences that can diffuse your differences. For example, with Mercury or Venus in Pisces, you'll have a natural understanding of your lover that will help smooth communication. With the Moon in any water sign, chances for compatibility are increased. This isn't an easy relationship, but can enrich your life if you can get past your differences in style.

ABOUT THE AUTHORS

RICK LEVINE When I first encountered astrology as a psychology undergraduate in the late 1960s, I became fascinated with the varieties of human experience. Even now, I love the one-on-one work of seeing clients and looking at their lives through the cosmic lens. But I also love history and utilize astrology to better understand the longer-term cycles of cultural change. My recent DVD, *Quantum Astrology*, explores some of these transpersonal interests. As a scientist, I'm always looking for patterns in order to improve my ability to predict the outcome of any experiment; as an artist, I'm entranced by the mystery of what we do not and cannot know. As an astrologer, I am privileged to live in an enchanted world that links the rational and magical, physical and spiritual—and yes—even science and art.

JEFF JAWER I'm a Taurus with a Scorpio Moon and Aries rising who lives in the Pacific Northwest with Danick, my double-Pisces musician wife, our two Leo daughters, a black Gemini cat, and a white Pisces dog. I have been a professional astrologer since 1973 when I was a student at the University of Massachusetts (Amherst). I encountered astrology as my first marriage was ending and I was searching for answers. Astrology provided them. More than thirty-five years later, it remains the creative passion of my life as I continue to counsel, write, study, and share ideas with clients and colleagues around the world.

ACKNOWLEDGMENTS

Thanks to Paul O'Brien, our agent, our friend, and the creative genius behind Tarot.com; Gail Goldberg, the editor who always makes us sound better; Marcus Leaver and Michael Fragnito at Sterling Publishing, for their tireless support for the project; Barbara Berger, our supervising editor, who has shepherded this book with Taurean persistence and Aquarian invention; Laura Jorstad, for her refinement of the text; and Sterling project editor Mary Hern, assistant editor Sasha Tropp, and designer Abrah Griggs for their invaluable help. We thank Bob Wietrak and Jules Herbert at Barnes & Noble, and all of the helping hands at Sterling. Thanks for the art and ideas from Jessica Abel and the rest of the Tarot.com team. Thanks as well to 3+Co. for the original design and to Tara Gimmer for the author photo.